W9-BRW-446

At David C Cook, we equip the local church around
the corner and around the globe to make disciples.
Come see how we are working together—go to
www.davidccook.org. Thank you!

DAVID **C** COOK
transforming lives together

What people are saying about …

Yes, No, and Maybe

"I love how Wendy reveals the biblical truth that God has so many wonderful plans for us, but we must learn to fight for His best with bold faith. *Yes, No, and Maybe* is the book you need to breathe fresh air into the weary places of your heart desperate for new life."

Lysa TerKeurst, *New York Times* bestselling author and president of Proverbs 31 Ministries

"I read a lot of books. After reading the first chapter of Wendy's new book, I texted her and said, 'I need this message.' And I've felt that way the entire way through. Wendy has such a gift to write in a way that immediately pulls you in but allows you to use practical application, along with biblical teaching. I felt convicted, challenged, and changed by the end. Make this your next Bible study!"

Nicki Koziarz, bestselling author, Bible teacher, and national speaker

"H. E. Fosdick said that preaching is 'personal counseling on a group scale.' In her newest book, Wendy similarly provides 'personal spiritual coaching' for a mass audience. Not merely an invitation to say 'Yes' to God, Wendy leads the reader through the sometimes gutwrenching process of saying 'No' to anything that distorts the image of Christ born in you as His new creation. But this is rewarded by experiencing the 'May Be' of 'Maybe,' as God transforms your understanding of the abundant life He desires for you. A book not merely to be read but experienced, as one writes his or her own last chapter—which will be met with both tears and celebration."

John Butler, chief operations officer for Baptist
State Convention of North Carolina

"Wendy Pope vulnerably shares from her experience and helps you feel encouraged and empowered as you say yes to what God's called you to do. She explores what it means to say no in different areas of your life, so you can be all God's called you to be. And she inspires your heart to hope for all the possibilities of abundant life in Christ. She not only gives you biblical insight into applying Scripture; she also provides practical steps for personal transformation. Her passion for you to know the Word of God inspires every lesson as you learn to say yes, no, and maybe."

Jill Monaco, speaker, coach, and
author of *Freedom Coach Model*

"In a world where we are judged by what we agree to and what we stand against, finding our reasons for what we say yes, no, and maybe to can help us draw closer to God, know Him better, and trust Him more completely. Join Wendy as she unpacks a journey to curating the life that God designed just for us."

Kathi Lipp, bestselling author of *The Husband
Project*, *Overwhelmed*, and *Clutter Free*

"Wendy writes in a comfortable, relatable way, with a strong gospel message and strong biblical explanation—and as a preacher, I know that isn't easy to do!"

Chris Justice, senior pastor of Lee Park Church

"Finally, a book that takes us out of the 'Is this as good as it gets?' mentality and transforms us so that we can experience the unbelievably, immeasurably more that God has in store for each Christian. Wendy's vulnerability and insight will encourage and excite women to get to know God and His Word. No matter where you are in your Christian walk with Jesus, *Yes, No, and Maybe* will dramatically change your relationship with God. Your life will never be the same!"

Linda Schoch

"Do you feel like you are a hot-mess Christian? You are not alone! Have you truly surrendered to the authority of Jesus? If Jesus is not already your magnificent obsession, after reading this book, your life will change! I could not put this book down!"

Jane Dean

"Wendy Pope welcomes the reader, who may feel that their current daily life is insignificant and unfulfilled, to experience the immeasurably more life that God desires for them. The reader is offered the opportunity to explore what their life could look like as they seek God and trust Him in a new and refreshing way."

Linda Leimone

"It's been said that the average person makes 35,000 decisions each day. No wonder we are run ragged, have no margin in our lives, and typically answer the common question 'How are you?' with one word: 'Busy.' Through practical insight, along with raw, honest, and heartfelt stories, Wendy shows us that we can have a life that is immeasurably more than we could ever imagine—while creating a schedule that allows us to be a part of it."

Shelley Summerville, P31 volunteer and book reviewer

"Wendy's love for the Lord shines through as she shares personal stories with warmth, humor, and vulnerability—making her message relatable and real for the reader. I love how she encourages and motivates with her words. This book will spark a fire inside of you to spread God's love!"

Jan Davis, reading teacher

"Wendy writes with a beautiful blend of humility, transparency, conviction, and boldness. Her message in *Yes, No, and Maybe* convicted me, challenged me, and encouraged me through God's Word to trust the God of immeasurably more. With truth and tenderness, Wendy draws us out of our comfort zones to grow our faith in Christ, consistently pointing us to Him and His Word."

Sharon Sloan

"What changes will you make to your life after reading *Yes, No, and Maybe*? Consider your 'yeses' more intentionally. Prioritize time in God's Word. Be more obedient, trusting, submissive, and faithful. And adjust your self-image."

Penny Sorokes

Yes, No, & Maybe

Living with the God of Immeasurably More

Wendy Pope

DAVID **C** COOK

transforming lives together

YES, NO, AND MAYBE
Published by David C Cook
4050 Lee Vance Drive
Colorado Springs, CO 80918 U.S.A.

Integrity Music Limited, a Division of David C Cook
Eastbourne, East Sussex BN23 6NT, England

The graphic circle C logo is a registered trademark of David C Cook.

The website addresses recommended throughout this book are offered as a
resource to you. These websites are not intended in any way to be or imply an
endorsement on the part of David C Cook, nor do we vouch for their content.

Details in some stories have been changed to protect
the identities of the persons involved.

Bible credits are listed at the back of this book.
The author has added italics to Scripture quotations for emphasis.

LCCN 2018938846
ISBN 978-0-7814-1356-5
eISBN 978-0-8307-7557-6

The Team: Wendi Lord, Laura Derico, Nick Lee, Jack Campbell, Susan Murdock
Cover Design: Amy Konyndyk
Cover Photo: Getty Images

Printed in the United States of America
First Edition 2018

1 2 3 4 5 6 7 8 9 10

072718

To Lysa
Thank you for saying yes to God.
Your yes changed my life.

Contents

Acknowledgments

To the Yes, No, and Maybe Focus Group: Penny, Contessa, Jane, Linda, Sharon, Shelley, and Jan. Thank you for the investment you made in the manuscript. Your feedback was more valuable than you know. I pray God's greatest and best on you and your family. Did you know I am writing a third book? Wanna read it?

To Tim Peterson: You took a chance on a first-time author and offered her a two-book contract. I missed you on the development and production of book 2 and would be remiss if I didn't give you a huge shout-out! Big blessings on your future.

To my team at David C Cook: I love my publishing family. Annette, I smile just thinking about you. The investment you have made and continue to make in me both personally and professionally has been a huge blessing. Laura, thank you for listening to those *Wait and See* teachings over and over again. You know my voice and have shaped this book into something special. Thank you for being generous with your wisdom. You helped me smooth out a few bumpy places. Amy, another breathtaking cover! It's soft and inviting. Wendi Lord, thank you for heading up our great team above, as well as Megan, Susan, Austin, and Jack. Here's to another movement of another book written and published for the glory of God and the growth of His people.

To Blythe Daniel: My agent extraordinaire! Thank you, thank you, and thank you. You always look after the best interests of your clients, and you always have time for your friends. I'm honored to be both. Having you on my team makes the future goals seem obtainable.

To Samantha: Wow, have we come a long way from the days of you editing my P31 devotions. Your love for the Word ensures my words uphold the Truth with honor and accuracy.

To Glynnis: You have invested so much time in my writing over the years. You have such a gift for constructive criticism. I know for certain I would not be publishing a second book without all the love you've poured into me and my writing. Thank you for always being for me.

To Scott, Blaire, and Griffin: You are my people, my first priority, and my partners in ministry … you are my ministry. If you haven't learned the principles of yes to God, no to self, and maybe to others, then the field test of this book has failed. My heart cries for each of you to know God intimately so that you may boldly make Him known to a lost and lonely world who desperately needs the hope He offers. Thank you for loving me as God wrote this message on my heart and polished it with the work His Spirit is teaching me to live it out. I love you more than words can say.

Foreword

I'll never forget the day I met Wendy Pope. It was my first day of work at Proverbs 31 Ministries. Working at a ministry was the last place I expected to find myself. You see, I'm a lawyer by training.

When my husband's job moved us from Texas to Charlotte, we decided rather than practice law, I'd stay home with the kids. But to help with finances, I sought out a part-time job. God opened a door for me at Proverbs 31.

On my first day, one of the gals gave me a quick tour and walked me to my desk, which was not only close to the desk across from me, it adjoined it. Three days a week working that close to someone I didn't know felt a bit uncomfortable for this girl who was used to her own office.

Little did I know that my new desk buddy, who happened to have my same first name, would become one of my dearest friends. Not only a friend, but a prayer partner, counselor, and woman who truly lives what she preaches.

That's what I love most about Wendy: what you see is what you get. She's the real deal. Gut honest, even when it hurts. I've walked with her for the last ten years through some of the very lessons she writes in the pages of this book.

Wendy's book brings us fresh insight from Paul's life that translates into life-transforming messages. Messages that examine the "yes-no-maybe" dilemmas we all experience. Through these three words, Wendy, in a practical way, equips us, chapter by chapter, to trade our unmet expectations, unfulfilled dreams, unanswered prayers, and unwanted circumstances for *the* life God created us for. For *the inconceivable, indescribable, abundant* life promised us in God's Word.

Wendy teaches that the life we've always dreamed of is one yes away. Freedom to walk in the fullness of the immeasurably more life God has for us begins with that first yes.

But it's not about rules and what we can and cannot do. It's about walking step by step with God, living in relationship with Him, and listening for His voice to know when to say yes, when to say no, and when to say maybe. With each step, we more willingly surrender our desires for God's. We trust Him more, so we obey Him more. Along the way, we begin to look less like the world and more like Jesus.

And something unique that sets this book apart from any other you've read is Wendy's invitation. She invites the reader—that's you and me—to write the final chapter! Chapter by chapter we apply what we learn, creating and defining our immeasurably more life— what it looks like and the steps we take to get there.

Accept Wendy's invitation. Take this journey. Invite the Holy Spirit to do His refining work in you and usher you into a life beyond anything you could ever ask or imagine. He is able!

Wendy Blight

Speaker

Author of *Living So That* and *I Am Loved*

Introduction

"What if this is as good as it gets?"

That's the question asked by the obsessive-compulsive novelist Melvin Udall (as portrayed by Jack Nicholson) in the movie *As Good as It Gets*. Melvin is a recluse who only leaves his New York City apartment when he *has* to go somewhere. He eats the same breakfast at the same table in the same restaurant every day. He repeatedly washes his hands, checks his locks fifteen times, uses plastic utensils when eating out, and never steps on cracks in the sidewalks. He has a general hatred and distrust for all people—until he develops a relationship with Carol, his regular waitress. Something about her makes Melvin want to be a better man. But sitting in his psychiatrist's waiting room, Melvin wonders, *What if this is as good as it gets?*

Though Melvin and I share very little in common, I can resonate with his cynical stance. Once upon a time, I uttered similar words myself. What about you—can you relate to Melvin?

Maybe life has worn you down. You attend church and even midweek Bible study. On the Sundays when you aren't greeting visitors, you're rocking babies in the nursery or rushing back and forth between services to sing in the choir or on the worship team. The other six days of the week are no less hectic. The laundry pile is endless. The family insists on eating dinner every night. Homework is hard. School projects are complicated. You feel like an unpaid Uber driver in overdrive, with ballet lessons for Susie on Tuesday, karate for Sam on Saturday, dental cleanings for everyone on Wednesday, and a visit to the veterinarian for Rover this afternoon. In exhaustion, you collapse into the worn-out easy chair and survey your life …

Or maybe debt is what keeps you up at night. Student loans loom. Jobs in your field of study aren't available. Working two part-time jobs to make ends meet, you still seem to run out of money before you run out of month. As you stare at your shrinking bank account, you examine your life …

Or maybe you feel like your life is on track, but you long for a companion. You serve joyfully at church and in the community. Your dream job is booming. And reading all the books on singleness is teaching you how to meet the right person by being the right person—but the dating site still has not found your perfect match. As you open yet another invitation to a wedding, you evaluate your life …

Whether we're stay-at-home moms or go-getting career women, devoted wives or single gals, we've all had those moments when we've been weighed down by the "uns" of life. These "uns" filter into our lives, no matter where we are or what we're doing:

*Un*met expectations: "I thought God would …"

*Un*fulfilled dreams: "Why didn't He …?"

*Un*answered prayers: "I long for God to …"

*Un*wanted situations: "If only …"

What is that old saying? *Been there. Done that. Got the T-shirt.* Is your T-shirt tattered and faded but still legible? My "uns" have faded in memory, though they're not forgotten. But the life I now enjoy with Christ has taught me to cease fixating on what *isn't* fulfilled and instead focus on what *is* taking place because of His grace.

THIRTEEN WORDS THAT CHANGED MY LIFE

The night did not differ from most other nights. I'd cooked dinner and cleaned up before my husband got home from work. Our kids, bathed and in their jammies, had headed to sleepy town already when Scott walked through the door. We exchanged our usual "How was your day?" banter before he headed upstairs to his man cave.

The words I had rehearsed all day were playing like a symphony in my head. It was time to have a talk with my man. Things had been silent between us for far too long. Something had to change. His overtime kept him away from our family. I was lonely, and raising the kids was hard work. Our children and I needed him home more, and I decided it was time to let him know that he needed to make some changes. I was poised and prepared for every comeback he could hurl at me—every comeback except one.

My heart pounded as I entered the room. I sheepishly sat down on the floor beside Scott and waited for just the right time to let him know how I was feeling. I asked questions as if I was interested in what he was doing. Then, when the forced conversation lulled, I lunged into my lengthy, well-prepared diatribe, ending with what I thought was a showstopper: "You don't act like you ever want to come home."

Scott paused for a moment before he spewed a comeback that all my rehearsing hadn't prepared me to hear. Much to my surprise, Scott had the real showstopper: "You don't make our house a place I want to come home to."

Hanging in the air were thirteen words that changed the course of my life forever.

Everything after that moment was a blur. I had no words to speak in defense of myself. No cute retorts or witty one-liners. Honestly, I can't even remember how the conversation ended. I only remember those thirteen stinging words.

"You don't make our house a place I want to come home to." Heavy, hurtful, convicting, and somewhat thought-provoking words. Was he right? Did I make our home unwelcoming to the very man who worked so hard to provide it? *Certainly not*, I reasoned with myself. *I clean, cook, and care for our children. He always has pressed clothes, clean underwear, and on most nights a hot meal.*

For days, my emotions fought with Scott's words. What he'd said messed with me in the worst—and best—way. Eventually the wrestling match ended; the words won. I hadn't decided yet to *agree* with my husband, but the thought of his words being remotely true jolted me to my core. After mulling over his words for several days, I had to admit there was truth in them. My heart wasn't happy, and therefore, my life wasn't happy. "For out of the overflow of the heart, the mouth speaks" (Luke 6:45 BSB).

Scott's words propelled me to change my heart. I wasn't sure how this metamorphosis was going to happen, but as Melvin had tried to be a better man for Carol, I wanted to try to be a better wife and mother for my family. In the pursuit to become what my family deserved, I cried out to God my version of Melvin's words: "Surely this isn't all there is, God. I've got so much life to live; this can't be as good as it gets. What do I need to do to fix this mess?"

On the surface, our house looked like a place Scott would want to come home to. But it didn't matter how things *looked* inside our four walls—what was in my heart and came out of my mouth were the things that created the unpleasant atmosphere. Snippy words. Angry responses. Long sighs of disappointment. Passive-aggressive behavior. All these affected my family and the tone of our home. Once I recognized this, I looked for the root of my negative actions. What I found was general unhappiness and numbness.

Asking ourselves *Is this as good as it gets?* digs deeper into the source of our troubled heart. This question doesn't mean we are ungrateful for Jesus's sacrificial death but implies our determination to get to the root of our discontent. It's not just about where we live, what kind of car we drive, or how much money we have in the bank. Our numbness is the result of "un" roots growing in our heart, choking the life out of joy. We succumb to the power of every unmet expectation, unfulfilled dream, unanswered prayer, and unwanted situation. The "I thought God would," "Why didn't He?," "I longed for God to," and "If only" scripts run on auto-play, and we don't know how to change the playlist. Our response to life becomes cynical and pessimistic. The roots grown out of numbness become deeper, the scripts play louder, and without realizing it, we begin operating on autopilot, running life's race, hurtling from one task to the next, all the while leaving behind an unpleasant atmosphere for those around us.

My race was stale. Each morning I'd plaster on a "today's a new day" face. The wear pattern of my shoes never changed—I ran the same path, dodged the same obstacles, and crossed the same finish line day in and day out. In all honesty, I was just going through the motions of a good Christian life. I was trying my best to do the right things that Christians should do. You know?—the *right* things:

- Have a relationship with God (of sorts)
- Know Jesus as your Savior (of course)
- Pray (sometimes)
- Be involved in activities at church (and make sure others see it!)
- Tithe (though giving cheerfully might be a stretch)
- Help the less fortunate (as long as it's not too inconvenient)
- Read your Bible (does falling asleep with it open count?)

The way I was living life was wearing me out. Maybe that's why I identified so closely with Melvin. He was trying so hard, but all his efforts seemed to be in vain. Melvin was ready for a change, and so was Wendy.

THIS IS *NOT AS GOOD AS IT GETS*

I have great news! You and I were created for more than mundane motions. This is *not* as good as it gets. What awaits us is *life with the God of immeasurably more*: "Now to him who is able to do immeasurably more than all we ask or imagine" (Eph. 3:20).

Let's see how great this great news really is by unpacking this New Testament verse with a few simple word studies. We will start with the phrase *immeasurably more*.

The apostle Paul's letter was written mainly to the Greeks in the city of Ephesus who had become followers of Jesus. The phrase *immeasurably more* comes from a compound Greek adverb: *hyperekperissou* (hoo-per-ek-pe-rees-soo'). If we break this word down to look at its roots, *hyper* (hoop-er') means "for the sake of, more and beyond."[1] *Perissos* (per-is-sos') means "exceeding some number, measure, rank or need," and (my favorite part of the definition) "over and above, more than is necessary."[2] Some Bible translators express the phrase as "super- abundantly more." God is able to do superabundantly more than we ask or imagine. This great news is getting greater, isn't it?

Paul wrote this letter to the believers in Ephesus to remind them of who they were in Christ—not Jews, not Gentiles, but one body. And they were no longer to get caught up in their old way of life—to get lost in some stale routine. Instead, they were to realize that they were made alive in Christ and that they had an all-access pass to the peace and power and joy and grace of our amazing, loving God.

That's why this letter, written so long ago, still speaks to us right now. The Ephesians had faced challenges. They had been discouraged. They were disappointed—in themselves and in others. This life follow- ing the King of Kings maybe didn't seem as royally awesome as they thought it might be. And this guy who had taught them about Jesus was now locked up for it.

Disappointments aren't fun to ponder, and painful scripts aren't easy to replay, but let's pause for a moment and consider your "uns." (I promise this little exercise will be worth it!) Right here, right now, we are gonna write new scripts. Are you ready? Remember the power you have access to: God can do *more than*. Feel this power: God can do *superabundantly, immeasurably more*.

*Un*met expectations? Say: "God will superabundantly exceed my expectations."

*Un*fulfilled dreams? Say: "God will superabundantly surpass my dreams."

*Un*answered prayers? Say: "God's answer will be superabundantly greater than I expect."

*Un*wanted situations? Say: "God's resolution will be superabundantly better than mine."

Now, read the list aloud. Do you feel the power of this awesome news!?

> **Even if your good is really good, your really good is not as good as it gets.**

Repeat the new scripts aloud. Let them marinate deep into your soul. God will transform your greatest disappointments and repair your most hurtful rejections. He wants to do this for you, and He can do this for you: "Now to Him who is able to do immeasurably more than all we ask or imagine." He gave His Son so you could have a life that is greater than the sum of your sorrows.

The *immeasurably more life* is

- Greater than the sum of your failures.
- Greater than the sum of your past experiences.
- Greater than the sum of your hopes.

- Greater than the sum of your accomplishments.
- Greater than the sum of your bank account.
- Greater than the sum of your titles and degrees.

Friend, even if your good is really good, your really good is *not* as good as it gets. With Christ, good gets better, better gets great, and great, well, gets extraordinary. The immeasurably more life is the extraordinary life. It's the life you've longed for but only dreamed of living.

Let's settle something before we move any further: because we live in a fallen world, we *will* experience numbness and the heartaches of "uns." But they *do not* have to have power over us. In *Yes, No, and Maybe*, we are going to trade our *un*met expectations, *un*fulfilled dreams, *un*answered prayers, and *un*wanted situations for an *in*conceivable and *in*describable life.

Our journey to living the immeasurably more life will begin in the book of Acts, where we will meet a man named Saul who had an unbelievable encounter with God. After this life-altering event, he became known as the apostle Paul. We will travel with him, read his letters to the early churches, and discover how to live the life Jesus died to give—the immeasurably more life.

In the how-tos, we will learn how and when to use three simple yet powerful words: *yes*, *no*, and *maybe*. Each of the three main sections of the book focuses on one word and its related theme:

- Yes Cultivates Trust
- No Invites Revelation
- Maybe Welcomes Freedom

A SPECIAL FEATURE

One of my favorite features of *this book* is the active role you have in our journey. *Yes, No, and Maybe* is a real-time, reader-participatory book. Your role is greater than a reader and a Bible-study-question answerer. (I'm pretty sure I made up that title, but I can, because I'm the author.) You are a participant in an expedition to discover the life you were meant to live.

Yes, No, and Maybe provides you with the opportunity to experience real-life change as you apply God's truth to your real-life circumstances. How? *You* write the final chapter!

Hold on. Did you just break out in a cold sweat? Are you already thinking of excuses not to participate? No worries. You and God will be the only ones who will read your answers.

At the close of each chapter is a section called Ask and Imagine. I provide writing prompts that summarize the teachings we learn in each chapter. After reading the prompt, you will turn to chapter 10, "My Immeasurably More Life," and respond.

Your participation starts now. "My Immeasurably More Life" is full of blank lines. There won't be a teacher with a red pen in hand, ready to correct misspelled words, incorrect grammar, and typographical errors. It's okay for the pages to be stained with tears as you pour out your heart to the God of immeasurably more. Or the pages may be filled with happy doodles as you dream of ways your life can bring God glory.

You may love the idea of writing in your book … or you may dislike it. If journaling on the pages of this book doesn't appeal to you, that's no problem. Feel free to write your thoughts and answers in a notebook or type them on your computer or phone—whatever works for you.

God's waiting to meet with you. He longs to intersect your hurts with His mercy, fill your emptiness with His love, and wash away your guilt with His grace. With God, life gets better and better. Your immeasurably more life awaits.

ASK AND IMAGINE

Turn to chapter 10, "My Immeasurably More Life," and make an honest list of the "uns" in your life. Then draw a line through each of them. Write out the new superabundantly scripts we created when studying Ephesians 3:20.

Section One

Yes Cultivates Trust

*For it is by grace you have been saved, through faith—and
this is not from yourselves, it is the gift of God.*

Ephesians 2:8

1

Obedience: Our First Yes

Okay. You may be dismayed by the title of chapter 1, particularly this one word: *obedience*. Maybe you even rolled your eyes and released a deep sigh when you read that word. In the introduction, you got all hyped up about the immeasurably more life, only to turn the page and read a word that sticks in your teeth like a kernel of popcorn.

Please don't put this book down. And please don't take it back to the store and ask for a refund.

Obedience and *obey* are not among popular Bible words like *grace*. Oh, we welcome God's grace. Then there's *mercy*. Don't we love God's mercy? We can't forget *cleansed, forgiven, washed away*, and *dearly loved*. We flock to these Bible words. But *obey*? Not so much. However, when we survey feel-good, inspirational words, we might consider that each word is experienced in its fullest when our heart is in alignment with God's—when we are obedient to Him. How would we respond to God's instructions if we knew the impact our obedience to God would have on the immeasurably more life we long to live? Saying yes to obedience cultivates trust—our trust in God as well as God's trust in us.

I'll go ahead and admit that I'm a rule follower. I haven't always loved or embraced regulations. But I've matured and come to understand that most rules are for the greater good. Speed limits and stop signs are put in place to keep drivers, bicyclists, and pedestrians safe. Imagine the chaos that would ensue with unrestricted speeds and no stop signs! As a former non-lover of rules, I now find security in knowing and following the expectations before me. A flood of joy fills me when I adhere to instructions, even those I don't like or understand.

I am the mom who clocked every minute of her teenagers' driving hours in order for them to receive their driver's licenses. Nope, I didn't fudge at all. The sign at the movie theater clearly states "No outside food," so no candy smuggling into the theater for me. When the hotel checkout time is at 10:00 a.m., we leave by 10:00 a.m.—even when no one is around to verify our on-time departure. Some women can make a dish with a little of this and a pinch of that. Oh, do I admire these women! My rule-abiding heart just won't let me ad lib in the kitchen. If the recipe calls for a teaspoon of oregano, I get the measuring spoon out and level it off.

> **Saying yes to obedience cultivates trust—our trust in God as well as God's trust in us.**

Some may say I have a problem. I get that. Really, I do. But for me, if I know the guidelines, I feel convicted that it is my responsibility to follow them.

However, when it comes to obeying God, that's a different story. Please tell me I'm not the only one who winces at the word *obey*. That word stirs up different reactions. *It's too hard. I really just want to live like I want to live. What exactly am I supposed to obey? Obedience brings me great joy!* And each of us, at any given time, has probably experienced each statement.

The bottom line is this: obedience makes our life in Christ come alive. The single most important yes you will ever say is when you accept God's invitation to eternal life.

OUR FIRST AND BIGGEST YES

Let's start at the beginning. As in "In the beginning"—that part of the Bible that starts the whole story, found in Genesis 1 and 2. God in all His creative genius established the whole world. From the first "Let there be" on day one, until the fashioning of Adam on day six, and rest on day seven, God laid out His plan for mankind. God enjoyed fellowship with Adam and Eve in His breathtaking garden. He provided everything they would ever need and protected them from what they didn't. God's good plan for mankind and the earth was set into motion. But one day Adam and Eve took it off the rails.

Adam and Eve disobeyed God (Gen. 2:16–17; 3:6–7), which severed their perfect connection with Him. This act of disobedience brought sin into the world and birthed our need for a Savior. Unless Adam's sin was paid for, we would be separated from God forever. "For God so loved the world, that He gave His only begotten Son, that whoever believes in Him shall not perish, but have eternal life" (John 3:16 NASB).

Jesus is sometimes referred to as the second Adam or the last Adam (see 1 Cor. 15:45). The first Adam represented the natural life, which was marred by passing sin from generation to generation. From him, all people have inherited a sin nature. Jesus represents the spiritual life. Jesus's birth, death, and resurrection didn't remove our sin nature. But His gift of salvation does give us a new, spiritual nature. It gives us the possibility of life without the power of sin reigning over us. Note the word *possibility*; we will revisit the concept later.

Let's go back to the Garden for a minute. God saw that everything He created was good, even the Tree of the Knowledge of Good and Evil. If God knew that having knowledge of good and evil wouldn't benefit Adam and Eve, then why would He create such a tree and tell Adam and Eve not to eat from it?

God could have made Adam and Eve do exactly what He wanted them to do, like a marionette controlling puppets by their strings. But God wanted the first family to *choose* to obey Him—to build a trust relationship with Him. He wanted them to look at the tree and say, "This tree is beautiful. The fruit looks delicious. I don't know why God said we can't have it, but I will trust and obey Him, even when I don't understand." But we all know that's not what happened.

The *possibility* of a Spirit-filled life, free from the pulling power of sin, is available to us. But we can't even see that possibility until we accept God's invitation for salvation—our first and biggest yes to God.

SIN, MEET SALVATION

Jesus's sacrifice on the cross is the bridge between sin and salvation. God's desire was to be in uninterrupted fellowship with His creation.

However, Adam and Eve's sin put a kink in that perfect plan. So God sent His Son to satisfy the debt of our sin. He died in our place to close the gap between mankind and the punishment of sin, which is death.

God invites us to be His sons and daughters through the free gift of salvation (see Rom. 6:23). No strings attached, no price to pay, and no good works necessary (see Eph. 2:8–9). Everyone, without exception, is invited to be part of God's family, to know and live with the God of immeasurably more, free from the power and penalty of sin.

At the tender age of seven, I accepted my invitation. The tub was filled with Mr. Bubble and my momma was helping me with my Saturday night bath. (We always got clean on Saturday for church on Sunday.) We started talking about Jesus. She explained salvation. I told her I wanted Jesus to live in my heart.

The next Sunday, I met with my pastor in his study. I remember it vividly. The room was big and filled with lots of books. The morning sun shone through the big window, and the smell of my pastor's Old Spice tickled my nose. Without hesitation, I hopped up into one of his big, comfy chairs, my legs hanging over the soft leather because they weren't long enough for my feet to touch the floor. It was intimidating and exhilarating at the same time. I felt so grown up.

Believing is an ongoing decision, not just a onetime event.

My pastor shared the plan of salvation as he read through a blue-and-white pamphlet. On the last page were two hills separated by a divide. He labeled one hill "God," the other hill "Wendy," and the divide "sin." With his black pen, he drew a cross connecting the two hills and wrote "Jesus." In my mind and heart, I crossed that bridge.

Then we prayed. The following Sunday, my chubby seven-year-old legs carried me down the aisle. I took my pastor's hand and made my private decision public. I believed in Jesus, and my sin met salvation on January 19, 1975. Everyone who believes Christ is Lord will be saved: "For I am not ashamed of the gospel, because it is the power of God that brings salvation to everyone who believes: first to the Jew, then to the Gentile" (Rom. 1:16).

The word *salvation* in the Greek is *sótéria* (so-tay-ree'-ah). It means "deliverance, preservation, safety, and salvation." *Helps Word Studies* defines *sótéria* like this: "God's rescue which delivers believers out of destruction *and into* His safety."[1] For what better promise of hope could we surrender our earthly life and eternal life? If we confess our sins—all our sins—"he is faithful and just and will forgive us our sins and purify us from all unrighteousness" (1 John 1:9). Our old self is made new: "This means that anyone who belongs to Christ has become a new person. The old life is gone; a new life has begun!" (2 Cor. 5:17 NLT).

> ***Every yes we offer God demonstrates our***
> ***present-tense trust in Him.***

Oh, and we can't ignore the word *believes* in Romans 1:16. I'm not normally a grammar geek—only a word nerd—but this is really good stuff. The Greek word for "believe" is *pisteuó* (pist-yoo'-o).[2] *Pisteuó* means to believe and to have faith in. This use of the word is a present-tense verb, an action taking place currently. But the word can also describe things that happened in the past or certain events that are planned to happen in the future.

Believing is an ongoing decision, not just a onetime event. Every yes we offer God demonstrates our present-tense trust in Him.

Accepting Jesus's free gift of salvation is the beginning of our trusting relationship with the God of immeasurably more. A yes to salvation brings about internal changes that make us rethink our way of living and motivate us to live fully for Christ (we will discuss this more in the next section of the book). Salvation is available to *anyone* who believes. And God is patient with people. His Spirit can change the hardest of hearts and redirect the lifestyle of the most stubborn and willful. There is no one God won't pursue and can't use—even a Jesus hater.

THE HARD-HEARTED CHRISTIAN HATER

About the same time as Jesus's birth in Bethlehem, another boy was born in Tarsus, a Roman province of Cilicia (modern-day Turkey): Paul, whose Roman name was Paulous Saulos. His parents were a prominent, wealthy, Jewish couple from the tribe of Benjamin, and they were Pharisees of the largest Judaic branch.

The Pharisees were a sect of individuals who perverted the law of Moses into a legalistic way of life, rather than embracing its security and protection. This dogma became embedded in Saul from the moment he could toddle around a tent. Judaism is a religion based on the law given to Moses by God. The keeping of the law was the most important duty a Jew or believing Gentile could fulfill as a member of the "covenant community" of believers.[3]

The prominence and wealth of Saul's family afforded him educational opportunities that most would only dare to dream of. According to the Jewish Mishnah, which is the oldest official compilation of Jewish oral laws (created after the Bible writings), a young boy is able to learn Scripture at the age of five, and that was exactly when Paul's training began. At twelve, he moved with his family to Jerusalem, where he continued his training under the well-known and esteemed Rabbi Gamaliel, who exposed him to a broad education in the law, philosophy, ethics, and classical literature.

From the outside, Saul had it all: a prestigious family heritage, scholastic achievements, and community recognition. We first meet him—full of himself—on the outskirts of town, standing witness to the stoning of a Christian named Stephen.

> At this they covered their ears and, yelling at the top of their voices, they all rushed at him, dragged him out of the city and began to stone him. Meanwhile, the witnesses laid their coats at the feet of a young man named Saul.
>
> While they were stoning him, Stephen prayed, "Lord Jesus, receive my spirit." Then he fell on his knees and cried out, "Lord, do not hold this sin against them." When he had said this, he fell asleep. (Acts 7:57–60)

Saul's Jewish roots ran deep. There was no compromise in his commitment to the law and practices of Judaism. Under no circumstance was he going to allow Christianity to flourish. Any teaching other than the law was heretical. Like Stephen, anyone who taught about faith in Jesus Christ had to be confronted and condemned.

No one is beyond God's reach, and everyone is savable.

Saul was a Christian hater of the worst kind. His murderous actions and staunch convictions would have given modern-day missionaries pause to pray in abundance before sharing Christ. In fact, many Christians these days would steer away from a man like Saul and write him off as a lost cause for the kingdom of God. But no one is beyond God's reach, and everyone is savable. Aren't you thankful for this truth? Just like God sees potential in you and me, He saw potential in Saul.

However, Saul didn't want just to contain Christianity; he wanted to eradicate from the world anything having to do with Jesus or the Christian faith. Stephen's stoning marked the beginning of Saul's mission: "But Saul began to destroy the church. Going from house to house, he dragged off both men and women and put them in prison" (Acts 8:3).

Persecution of the church ran rampant in Jerusalem. Christians scattered, and news spread like wildfire far and wide of Saul's aggressive approach to believers of the Way. (The Way is the name Christ followers were referred to in Scripture. See Acts 9:1–2.) But Saul's tactics didn't stop the advancement of the early church, which made him even more determined to hate Jesus and His followers.

In an effort to take his persecution to a higher level, Saul asked Caiaphas the high priest for permission to travel to Damascus. His intent was to find men and women who followed Jesus and take them to prison in Jerusalem.

Let's put a paper clip on this page of the story for a minute and think about the why. Why was Saul so set on persecuting Christians?

There was great hostility between the Jews, converted Jews, and Gentile Christians. The conflict involved the concept of following the law— following the one true God of Moses—and the message of the gospel of Jesus, who claimed to be the Son of God. It is apparent that Stephen's preaching in a Greek synagogue about salvation through Jesus set Saul off. However, Saul's family and religious beliefs didn't teach him to have such a profound hatred for Christians, nor did it teach him to kill. So why did he advocate and encourage murder? Because he was born with a sin nature.

All the religious training in the world won't remove our sin nature. The sin nature rises up and oozes out of all of us. If it's not contained, it can affect even a little girl who is about to have her first sleepover with her best friend ...

We were both four years old when Christie and I played under the magnolia trees at Hickory Grove United Methodist Church, and she picked *me* to be her very best friend. In many ways, this decision directed the course of my life, but we will save those stories for another day. Part of being Christie's best friend included slumber parties at each other's homes. The excitement of our first sleepover was too much for my eager heart to bear. I couldn't wait to spend time with my new bestie, so I slipped into her classroom to begin our weekend together early.

It was logical to my mind that since I was sleeping over at Christie's house, I should stay in her classroom rather than go to my room—where I belonged—with Mrs. Knowland and Mrs. Highly. I was sitting in my "rightful" place (as I thought), beside my bestie, when her teacher Mrs. Greene asked why I was not in my *own* classroom. Without stuttering or stammering, my pink lips stated an eloquent, well-spoken lie: "Since

I am sleeping over at Christie's house tonight, Mrs. Knowland and Mrs. Highly said I could stay in here today."

Yes, I told that lie and went right back to what I was doing, never noticing that Mrs. Greene left the room to verify my tall tale. You can probably guess what happened next.

My teacher promptly and abruptly escorted me down the hall to my classroom. Rather than playing on the playground that sunny afternoon, I had the pleasure of sitting in the "principal's" office (aka, a hard chair beside the secretary in the church office, but still very scary). Did I learn my lesson about lying? For that day and in that moment, yes, but it wouldn't be the last time I would sin.

No one had to teach me how to lie. Adults taught me how to tie my shoes, make my bed, and ride a bike without training wheels. Other children taught me how to play tag and skip rope. Yet, as a young child, I knew how to tell a fib all by myself. I sinned on my own accord—and in a church preschool no less! Because of Adam's original sin in the Garden, all of his descendants (that's us) inherited a propensity to sin. We need an encounter with the Savior to help us not give in to temptation. Just like the Savior met me in the pastor's study, the Savior met Saul on a dusty road between Jerusalem and Damascus.

WHEN THE PERSECUTOR MET THE PERSECUTED

With official papers in hand and a regiment of men by his side, Saul readied himself for the 6-day, 130-mile journey to Damascus. He was in full pursuit to put an end to the Christianity craziness. In all his zeal and fury, I feel quite certain that Saul never considered that he himself was being pursued.

It's often in the unexpected moments that we
receive more than we expect from God.

Just about a mile or so from his destination, the pursued met the Pursuer in a bizarre and extraordinary way. The persecutor met the Persecuted. Saul met Jesus. God seeks His own, whether they're in a sycamore tree, like Zacchaeus; in the hull of a boat, like Jonah; or at a well in Samaria, like the woman with many husbands. God pursues His people. Saul had no idea that his immeasurably more life was going to begin while on a mission to steal the immeasurably more life from so many. "As he neared Damascus on his journey, suddenly a light from heaven flashed around him" (Acts 9:3).

Suddenly. Unexpectedly. Without warning. A light flashed from heaven. We know by reading Acts 22:6, another account of Saul's Damascus road moment, that the encounter occurred at midday. We'd expect the sun to be brilliant at noon, but we wouldn't anticipate a light brighter than the sun to blaze from heaven (Acts 26:13). The light was so bright that Saul and his brigade fell to the ground to protect their eyes. It's often in the unexpected moments that we receive more than we expect from God.

The encounter with sudden, unexpected light wasn't all that Saul and his companions experienced. Out of the piercing flash of light spoke a voice that everyone heard but only Saul could understand (see Acts 22:9). Jesus, in some manifestation of His glory, appeared to Saul. Without beating around the bush, He asked a question as piercing as the light that had blinded Saul's eyes: "Saul, Saul, why do you persecute me?" (Acts 9:4).

The proof of a Damascus road experience isn't whether someone hears us say a prayer but how we live our life after saying yes.

Jesus made sure that Saul had no doubt whom the message was intended for. With deep sentiment Jesus repeated Saul's name. Fear-stricken, with his eyes clinched, and his face buried, Saul dared to address the voice: "Who are you, Lord?" (Acts 9:5). Without hesitation, Jesus identified Himself and told Saul to get up and head into the city. The men stumbled to their feet and assisted Saul, because he still could not see. Totally bewildered, they walked through the city gate.

God used Ananias, a man from Damascus, to restore Saul's sight and nurse him back to health (Acts 9:17–19). Scripture does not record Saul repenting, or reciting a "sinner's prayer," or meeting with a priest to hear the plan of salvation. Saul met his Pursuer, and his heart said, "Yes"—the first and biggest yes of his life. The proof of a Damascus road experience isn't whether someone hears us say a prayer but how we live our life after saying yes. As believers, we do repent, and we do publicly confess Christ, but that mark of Christianity is in the fruit we bear over our lifetime, not during a onetime event like walking the aisle or praying with a pastor.

"Saul spent several days with the disciples in Damascus. At once he began to preach in the synagogues that Jesus is the Son of God" (Acts 9:19–20). Notice the words *at once*. Saul wasted no time living fully for God. His new life began when his eyes were blinded and Jesus spoke to his heart. I love the way Bible expositor and preacher Alexander Maclaren reports Saul's heart change:

Paul's Christianity meant a radical change in his whole nature. He went out of Jerusalem a persecutor, he came into Damascus a Christian. He rode out of Jerusalem hating, loathing, despising Jesus Christ; he groped his way into Damascus, broken, bruised, clinging contrite to His feet, and clasping His Cross as his only hope. He went out proud, self-reliant, pluming himself upon his many prerogatives, his blue blood, his pure descent, his Rabbinical knowledge, his Pharisaical training, his external religious earnestness, his rigid morality; he rode into Damascus blind in the eyes, but seeing in the soul, and discerning that all these things were, as he says in his strong, vehement way, "but dung" in comparison with his winning Christ.[4]

We are all born spiritually blind. We all grope through life searching for our story until our Pursuer invites us into His. Every soul saved has a Damascus road experience that's just waiting to be told. Your story may not be as spellbinding as Saul's, but it is no less significant to God.

Maybe as you are reading Paul's story you are reminded to pray for someone you know who isn't saved. Perhaps you may have read Saul's story and realized you don't have a Damascus road story of your own. And after reading my story and Saul's, you hear a voice from heaven speaking to your heart or feel a tugging at your heart that you've never felt before. You've had enough of the spiritual blindness and groping through life. You want today to be your day, the day of your salvation, your very own Damascus road experience.

Our focal verse for this first section of the book is Ephesians 2:8, "For it is by grace you have been saved, through faith—and this is not from yourselves, it is the gift of God." The invitation of salvation is being extended to you from God. God sent His only Son, Jesus, to cover the separation sin has caused between you and God.

We are all born spiritually blind. We all grope through life searching for our story until our Pursuer invites us into His.

In the space below, draw two hills. Write your name on the top of one hill and God's name on the top of the other hill. Label the space between the hills "sin." Now draw a cross connecting the two hills and write "Jesus" on the cross.

Oh, won't you open your beautiful gift of salvation today?

Perhaps you are thinking, *Salvation sounds wonderful, but you don't know what I've done. God surely wouldn't invite me, would He?* Yes, He would, and He does. Jesus invited Saul, a Jesus-hating, Christian-killing Pharisee. Jesus invited His disciples, a group of cowards, extortionists, and traitors. Jesus invited me, a liar and deceiver. And Jesus invites you. Jesus invites *you*. He extends His invitation to you in John 3:16, "For God so loved the world that he gave his one and only Son, that whoever believes in him shall not perish but have eternal life." You are a *whoever*.

Tell God that you are sorry for your sins and that you are thankful for His invitation to live eternally with Him. With your mouth, tell Him you believe He is Lord. In your heart, believe that Jesus rose from the dead and that salvation is yours forever (see Rom. 10:9). Step confidently into the life Jesus died to give you. And like Saul, *at once* begin to live fully for God as we learn how to do that in our journey together … and tell someone. If you don't have someone to tell, tell me: My contact information is in the back of the book. I'd love to celebrate with you.

NEW LIFE, NEW NAME

Everyone has a name, and every name has a meaning. My name is Wendy, pronounced Wen-dee. Its origin is English and means "friend." The name was created for the heroine in James Barrie's play *Peter Pan*.

Earlier, I introduced you to Saul by his full name, Paulous Saulos Paulus. *Saul* is derived from Hebrew and means "desired" or "asked for." *Paulus*, or *Paul*, is Greek in origin and means "small" or "humble." Following his personal encounter with Jesus, Saul *desired* to be identified as Paul. He no longer wanted to be known, but to make known the only one worth knowing—Jesus.

Our decision to follow Christ has the potential (I'll expound on the word *potential* later in the journey) to completely change us from the inside out. God longs to work in us through the power of His Holy Spirit to transform our life so that we can be His witness to the world. However, until we are standing on a solid foundation of faith, our old identity, things we used to do that pleased our flesh, will wrestle with our new identity, the thing we know we should do that pleases God.

Saul realized this truth. He knew himself as *desired*, and others knew him as *desired*. And moreover, others knew him as a murderer, God hater, provoker, and powerful evildoer. God changed his life, and Saul chose to go by his other name so he could live out his calling. Dual Hebrew and Greek names were commonplace in this day. One reason Saul may have chosen to drop *Saul* was because *Paul* was a less regal name (think of King Saul in the Old Testament). With a more common name, he could totally immerse himself in his role as the "apostle to the Gentiles": "I am talking to you Gentiles. Inasmuch as I am the apostle to the Gentiles, I take pride in my ministry" (Rom. 11:13). You see, we live out the name we call ourselves.

My son, Griffin, is fun loving, hardworking, and knows so much about so much. Once, when he was around eight, he collected scrap wood from our neighbor's building project. He used the remnants to build his own little house, complete with a floor, a front door, a window, and a roof with shingles. When I asked Griffin how he knew how to build such a structure, he responded, "I was born knowing." I stood back in awe of his construction project and his confidence in growing into a young man. What I couldn't see behind his wide smile, however, were the doubt and feelings of failure he struggled with in other areas of life. He hid these nagging thoughts when he talked with me and

Scott, so I never saw doubt and failure creep into his young mind, or his witness about Christ.

> *We live out the names we call ourselves, but through*
> *our salvation we are given new names.*

When did doubt creep in? How did the weight of failure climb on his back? Perhaps these things happened on the playground when he didn't catch the football as well as the other boys. Maybe they plagued him when he noticed his grades weren't as good as other students'. Though fully aware of his salvation in Christ and a young man now, Griffin's old identity, doubt, and failure continue to wrestle with his new identity, one of no shame or condemnation. He's learning to live with his new names and to take on a new identity.

I'm not a stranger to Griffin's type of struggle; maybe you aren't either. For most of my life, I called myself negative names. We live out the names we call ourselves, but through our salvation we are given new names. When we live by our new names, we experience our new life.

God's Word says you're His chosen child, wholly and dearly loved—yet someone else gets the job you are more qualified for and you identify with *rejected* instead. "Therefore, as God's chosen people, holy and dearly loved, clothe yourselves with compassion, kindness, humility, gentleness and patience" (Col. 3:12).

You select the "I am fearfully and wonderfully made" graphic for the lock screen of your phone, but when you look in the mirror, you identify more closely with *ugly* and *unworthy*. "I praise you because

I am fearfully and wonderfully made; your works are wonderful, I know that full well" (Ps. 139:14).

You sing, "I know You've cast my sin as far as the East is from the West,"[5] but you identify better with *condemned*. "As far as the east is from the west, so far has he removed our transgressions from us" (Ps. 103:12).

I WAS	I AM
Guilty	Forgiven
A Failure	Redeemed
Shameful	Holy
Cursed	Blessed
Unwanted	Chosen
A Sinner	Blameless
Abandoned	Adopted
A Beggar	An Heir

Review the lists above and feel free to add to them. Take your pen and cross through every old name you've called yourself. Put a star beside every new name. Thank God for renaming you. The next time one of your old names tries to set up a rematch with your new names, picture yourself crossing through the old and starring the new.

Oh, friend, let's call ourselves by our real names: *forgiven, redeemed, holy, blessed, chosen, blameless, adopted,* and *heir*. We live out the names we are called, so let's call ourselves by the right names. Let's desire to make His name known and allow the Spirit to do His work in us so that we can be His witnesses to the world.

AND WHAT WAS THAT ABOUT OBEDIENCE?

Let's remove the paper clip and pick up Paul's story on the Damascus road. We've gone through this story but have yet to read the word *obey*. Paul accepted the invitation to live for Jesus, but where in his story of conversion to Christianity did Paul say, "Lord, I will obey you"? Unless we take a deeper look at his response to Jesus, we will miss his commitment to obey God. Saul, the Christian killer, hears a loud voice, is suddenly blinded by a bright light, and falls down. With his face in the dirt he asks, "Who are you, Lord?" (Acts 9:5).

> *The immeasurably more life extends beyond*
> *Christ's accomplished work on Calvary.*

Paul's commitment to obey is found tucked in the meaning of the Greek word for *Lord*. *Kurios* (koo'-ree-os) means "ruler, master, one who exercises authority."[6] To accept and acknowledge Jesus as Lord means to obey or submit to His authority. As Saul stood to his feet and headed toward Damascus, he surrendered his will to Jesus, declaring to obey Him.

Jesus identified Himself, "I am Jesus, whom you are persecuting" (Acts 9:5). *Jesus* means "Yahweh saves" (or "Yahweh is salvation").[7] We acknowledge and surrender to God's authority when we call Him Lord.

This idea of surrender is where the rubber meets the road. The immeasurably more life extends beyond Christ's accomplished work on Calvary. It's more than accepting His free gift of salvation. The immeasurably more life follows the example of Paul: the giving up of our wants, whims, and wishes in order to obey the will of God. You may accept the free gift of salvation, ensuring your eternity, but if you never surrender to His lordship, you won't experience the life that the God of immeasurably more has to offer you. And you may find yourself asking, "Is this as good as it gets?"

Maybe you are new to the idea of obeying God, and giving up your will for His will seems a little over the top. Perhaps you are a little apprehensive about trusting Him with the everyday affairs of your life. I get it. Really, I do. I lived most of my Christian life leaning on my understanding, living my way, and keeping my pew warm on Sunday. But all that changed when, in my early thirties, I was confronted with how poorly my plan was working out.

Do you remember where my story started? Those thirteen words— "You don't make our house a place I want to come home to"—that pierced my heart? After Scott said them, I lowered my face to the ground and asked God to help me fix my messed-up life. Like Saul with his face down in the dirt before heaven, I knew I had to make Jesus the Lord of every area of my life. My first yes when I was a little girl secured my salvation. But the next yes of my full surrender to God's will and His Word as an adult, as a wife, and as a mother ushered me into a life beyond anything I could have asked for, thought of, or imagined. I still live with unmet expectations, unfulfilled dreams, unanswered prayers, and unwanted situations, but my relationship with God through Jesus makes it possible to live fully in spite of the "uns."

Jesus wants to be more than our Savior. He wants to be Lord of our life—directing our decisions, guiding our steps, calming our fears, enjoying our company, inhabiting our praise, and showering us with blessings from His bountiful riches. Total surrender to God and the work of His Word aren't for the faint of heart. There are obstacles along the way and an enemy who seeks to impede our progress. It's through surrender that we experience God, and it's through our experience with Him that our trust in Him grows. Saying yes cultivates trust. Trust empowers us to overcome the obstacles that stand in the way of our living with the God of immeasurably more.

ASK AND IMAGINE

Turn to chapter 10. Write about your Damascus road experience. And if you haven't had such an experience, write about where you are with your belief in God right now. End the section by listing every one of your new names. When did your sin meet Jesus's salvation? What is your new name?

If you think you might be ready to take the next step toward knowing and accepting Jesus Christ as your personal Savior, the best thing to do is to get involved with a local church family. The Billy Graham Evangelistic Association also has some great resources to help you take the next step in your faith, including the website PeaceWithGod.net and their church-finding tool at https://churches.goingfarther.net.

2

Obstacles to Yes

If yes cultivates trust, and we want a trust relationship with God, then what keeps us from continually saying yes to Him? Is it our *want to*? "I *want to* obey God, but I'm not sure I'll *want to* do what He will ask me to do." Perhaps it's our *willpower*. We want to obey Him, but we're not sure we *will* have the *power* to accomplish our assignment. Or maybe it's our *worth*. "I'm just not *worth it*. I've done so many things wrong. How could God want me to be a part of His great kingdom plans?"

Sometimes we are our own biggest obstacle to growing in Christ and living a life of obedience.

Have these thoughts run through your mind when you felt prompted by the Lord to step out in obedience? Sometimes we are our own biggest obstacle to growing in Christ and living a life of obedience. I've had the "pleasure" of hurdling over all these obstacles myself, and I have the scraped knees to prove it. Truth be told, my knees stay a bit sore at times when I still allow myself to stumble over these excuses. But as I've grown in my faith, and as I continually study and live out God's Word, I've come to know that He who began a good work in me is faithful to complete it (see Phil. 1:6). My job is to be faithful to cooperate with Him.

FINDING MY *WANT TO*: THE OBSTACLE OF SELF

Paul established his *want to* right away. He wanted to stay committed to the cause of Christ, and he did. Through rejection, physical beatings, and imprisonment, he remained dedicated to his purpose. What an awesome way to be remembered! We have so much to learn from Paul.

We left our friend and his small militia standing on the road, stunned, and covered in dust, close to his destination, the city of Damascus. Paul acknowledged Jesus as *Kurios*: ruler, master, and one who exercises authority. This acknowledgment set his *want to* in the right direction.

Let's closely examine the next moments and days of Paul's (we'll call him Paul from here on out) life: "Now get up and go into the city, and you will be told what you must do" (Acts 9:6).

> Saul got up from the ground, but when he opened his eyes he could see nothing. So they led him by the hand into Damascus. (Acts 9:8)

> Immediately, something like scales fell from Saul's eyes, and he could see again. He got up and was baptized. (Acts 9:18)

> At once he began to preach in the synagogues that
> Jesus is the Son of God. (Acts 9:20)

What central theme in Paul's behavior do you recognize? Paul responded to God's authority by continually saying *yes* from the moment he accepted Jesus as Savior and surrendered to His lordship.

Paul didn't debate within himself or with other Christians whether he should or should not be baptized. He didn't pause and ponder his roadside conversation with Jesus. He immediately submitted to the leadership and authority of Jesus—period. The end.

The moment Paul responded *yes* to God, his old nature—former thoughts and actions—was replaced by a new nature and the possibility of new ways of thinking and acting. (Remember when we noted the word *possibility* in chapter 1? I promise we will address the mystery of this word, and how it relates to the immeasurably more life, in the "*No* Invites Revelation" section.) Perhaps Paul fondly recalled his radical change in Damascus, and his eager desire to be a different person, when he wrote these words to the church in Corinth: "Therefore, if anyone is in Christ, he is a new creature; the old things passed away; behold, new things have come" (2 Cor. 5:17 NASB). Paul embraced his new nature with direct obedience to God's ways; this is something I wish I could say I have done.

THE FADED SMELL OF OLD SPICE

In January of 1975, I became a new creation when I received Jesus as my Savior. The years following my Damascus road experience were filled with Sunday school, church choir, Vacation Bible School, youth group, church sports, and church services, every time the doors were open. As I grew up, the excitement that had once pumped through my heart when I had sat in the leather chair and watched my pastor draw the cross between the two hills waned, and the smell of his Old Spice faded.

Despite all my church activities, I never really embraced my new nature that I'd inherited as a Christ follower. You see, I had *invited* Jesus to be my Savior, but I had not *surrendered* to His lordship and authority. By God's grace, I had stumbled my way through a half-hearted relationship with Him through my teens and twenties. That all came to a halt the day I sat on the floor with my legs crossed in front of my husband, subject to those thirteen piercing words: "You don't make our house a place I want to come home to." Our home was filled with tension instead of peace, anger instead of joy, and animosity instead of love. If I had to be honest, it wasn't a place I wanted to be either.

Soon after that life-changing conversation with Scott, I realized that if I wanted our home to be a place we wanted to be, my new nature needed to obey my new authority. Like it was for Paul, things began to change when I made the decision to submit to Jesus as *Kurios*.

When we embrace God's truth, our desire for safety supersedes our old nature's attempts to stray from God's best.

Some people buck authority. They don't want to be told what to do, by God or any human, because of past experiences in abusive relationships or with enduring harsh rules and restrictions. But God's boundaries, rules, and instructions create a safe place for us to dwell. God's idea of safe is not our idea of safe. This is a place where our trust in Him grows.

Paul's obedience led him to be shipwrecked, beaten, imprisoned, and bitten by a snake. Now, it's unlikely such things will happen to us; however, we have to be aware that we will not escape persecution. We don't have to be shackled to fear. We can take comfort in the certainty that God is always with us. "Be strong and courageous. Do not be afraid or terrified because of them, for the LORD your God goes with you; he will never leave you nor forsake you" (Deut. 31:6). The safest place for us to be is in the center of God's will, following Him in obedience.

When we embrace God's truth, our desire for safety supersedes our old nature's attempts to stray from God's best. When Jesus instructed Paul to "get up and go," Paul immediately "got up and went." Jesus's instructions were clear, and Paul didn't waver in giving the correct response.

How do you respond to God? Is your *want to* followed by "But, God …"? When we hesitate to obey God and when we question His commands, we are trusting more in ourselves than in Him. The obstacle of self is overcome when we make adjustments to our *want to* and learn to obey God without a pause, cause, or clause.

PAUSES, CAUSES, AND CLAUSES

Obedience without a pause needs little explanation. Scripture is full of folks who did not delay in obeying God. It's what Paul did when God met him on his way to Damascus. Abraham demonstrated immediate obedience when God said, "Go from your country, your people and your father's household to the land I will show you" (Gen. 12:1). Noah built the ark (see Gen. 6:13–22), and Elijah approached King Ahab to prophesy a drought (see 1 Kings 17:1), both without a pause. These heroes of the faith lived lives surrendered to God and had perfectly working *want tos*.

Obey without delay; this is the best way. It's fun to have little mottoes like this as reminders to follow God. But sometimes they're not so cute when we have to put them into action.

I'll be the first to admit, trusting God through obedience can be fearsome because we don't know what He will ask us to do. Building trust works like receiving money. Each time we are given funds, we deposit the money into our bank account, where it remains until we need it. Our Memory Bank of Faith works the same way. As we obey, we experience God's faithfulness. We deposit His acts of faithfulness in our bank; then, when He asks us to do something we don't understand, or maybe don't want to do, we can make a withdrawal from our Memory Bank and confidently adjust our *want to*. We have experienced His faithfulness and know that what He has asked us to do is completely trustworthy—even if it involves something unexpected.

Obey without delay; this is the best way.

This has happened to me on several occasions, once even at a drive-through window while ordering lunch. It had been a long drive, and my stomach was growling like a bear. Since I am a don't-stop-until-you-get-home driver, I decided to enjoy the drive-through dining experience. I spoke my order into the bulky box, drove around the building, and received my meal from a kind lady. Before I drove away, she said, "I just love your scarf!"

May I press pause and chase a squirrel for a moment? This is one of my favorite things about being a woman. It doesn't matter where you are; if you are wearing something cute, a woman you don't know will squeal a compliment to you. I somehow doubt the same type of exchange happens between men in an auto-parts store or in the club-house at the golf course.

With an "Aw, thank you," I organized myself to drive away. But I felt the Spirit nudge me to give the woman my scarf. Rather than imme-diately obeying without a pause, and expressing total disregard for the patrons behind me, I took my sweet time and put up an argument. *Why, Lord? She doesn't need this scarf. It won't match what she is wearing. Please. No. It's my favorite.* Despite my stalling, I eventually came to terms with the fact that my old nature was not going to win over my new nature. I obeyed what I had felt encouraged by God to do, though I did not do so with as happy a heart as I should have. Like yanking a bandage off a wound, I pulled my scarf from around my neck and politely handed it to the cashier. "Here, I'd like you to have it."

I was secretly hoping she'd say, "Oh no, I can't," so I could then get credit for the obedience (pitiful, I know). But she smiled and said, "Thank you so much." I drove away with my food and without my scarf. The sacrifice of my scarf was nothing compared to what I'd deposited in my Memory Bank of Faith. When we surrender to *Kurios*, He will provide opportunities to exercise our faith and fill our bank.

Let's fast-forward a few months after my drive-through experience to a grocery-store encounter. My shopping cart was full, but fortu-nately, the line wasn't. My cashier wore a smile, and we exchanged light banter. This had all the makings of a painless checkout process. In order to expedite my checkout, I bagged the items and placed the bags in my cart as she quickly ran them over the scanner. As the woman handed me my receipt, she said, "I love your necklace." *(Really?)* Because I had recently experienced this *give-it-to-her* nudging, I knew exactly what to do. Without a word, I unhooked the clasp and placed the necklace around her neck. "Thank you. I'd love for you to have it."

> **You see, the trust exchange works both ways. God wants us to be certain that we can trust Him, and He wants to see that He can trust us.**

You might be thinking, *If obedience means giving away my favorite things, then I'm not sure I want to participate.* For the record, God doesn't ask me to give away everything for which I receive a compliment. He used these opportunities to help me test my commitment to His authority and my love for Him. It was important for me to know how serious I was about fixing my *want to* and serving God as *Kurios.* You see, the trust exchange works both ways. God wants us to be certain that we can trust Him, and He wants to see that He can trust us to obey without hesitation.

Our confidence in obedience without pause grows as our knowledge of God's Word increases. The Holy Spirit nudges your heart to help a senior adult move her groceries from her cart to her car. You align the nudging with God's Word, "Let each of you look not only to his own interests, but also to the interests of others" (Phil. 2:4 ESV); and with assurance, without delay, you help her.

As I began to naturally respond to God with *yes,* I realized the scarf and the necklace and material items in general didn't mean nearly as much to me as obeying God without a pause. I wrestled with my initial reactions and desires to obey. I was tempted to hold on to my wishes rather than harness myself to God's ways. It's okay to wrestle with our reactions, but our final response should always be *yes*.

> ### *Our confidence in obedience without pause grows*
> ### *as our knowledge of God's Word increases.*

When God trusts us with an assignment, we can learn to trust Him with the outcome. He fills the emptiness we think we will experience by giving something away with His nearness, love, and pleasure. As I learned that obedience without a pause was the best and only response I should give God, my bank began to fill with the joy and peace of God's presence and goodness. It's a good thing too, because I was about to make a big withdrawal.

Sometimes God asks something big of us when we least expect it. Sometimes even in the middle of Sunday worship.

My normal Sunday seat faced the congregation from the choir loft. I was minding my own business, praising my Jesus, when the unexpected happened. *No, Lord. I can't. No one else is walking to the altar to bow. What will people think of me? This isn't the time in the service we go to the altar; that's at the end of the service.* The songs ended. The choir left the loft. I did not say *yes*.

The next Sunday was a repeat. Same scenario. Same assignment. Same response. As the week went on, my weight of disappointment was heavy. Oh, how my spirit grieved that my answer to God was *no*. In my conviction, I confessed my sin and received forgiveness.

The following Sunday was a repeat. Same scenario. Same assignment. Different response. *Yes, God. I will NOT follow the schedule in the bulletin and the expectation of others. I will leave the safety of this choir loft and bow before You in praise. I will sing praises to You, my audience of one, in a sanctuary full of people who might think I'm weird. Yes! Yes! Yes!*

I sensed eyes staring at me as I left my place of comfort. When I kneeled to worship, I was alone. When I stood to return to my place, others stood with me. While I had been kneeling, many others had joined me at the altar to share their praise to God and to pray. This beautiful moment was a deposit in my bank. The pleasure of God is greater than the fear of man's reactions. Tears are puddling in my eyes as I relive this moment with you. Even now, years later, the act of obedience, even if delayed, is palatable. There are times when obedience makes His Spirit almost touchable.

It's critical to remember that obedience without a pause is a process—a process full of mistakes, regrets, and misgivings. Even with banks full of His faithfulness, there will be times we will want to obey, but we will not. Don't be discouraged. Lavish yourself in His endless grace that forgives, and intently listen to His Spirit as He continues to beckon you. Then, when the next assignment comes, your response will be *yes!* The more you say *yes*, the more you will want to say *yes*. Fill your bank!

We can't expect God's faithfulness to follow selfish-based obedience.

Another way our *want to* is adjusted is to obey God without a cause. It should be our delight to offer God continual yeses without expecting anything in return from Him. However, there will be times when we desire for God to move in a mighty way, yet He seems to be taking His time. Rather than waiting well, we try to rush God with acts of obedience, as if we could twist His arm. We suddenly start doing all the "right things" that we should have been doing all along. We read our Bible each day, pray more, and help those in need. In other words, we get "God conscience." We start obeying His Word only for the cause of God moving on our behalf. I like to call this "pulling an Eddie Haskell."

Eddie Haskell was a fictional character on the 1950s television show *Leave It to Beaver*. The sitcom revolved around the Cleaver family: parents, Ward and June; an older son named Wally; and a younger son named Theodore (aka Beaver). Eddie was Wally's friend and quite a trickster. He had a reputation for getting into all manner of mischief. He would clown around with Wally and the other boys, but when Eddie would talk to Wally's parents, he would put on the charm. "Yes, ma'am, Mrs. Cleaver. No, sir, Mr. Cleaver. My, you look pretty today, Mrs. Cleaver." You get the picture. Eddie did the right thing only when he wanted the adults not to know he had done the wrong thing. His motives were deceptive. Is it possible we could have deceptive motives as well?

We can't expect God's faithfulness to follow selfish-based obedience. The Bible gives a warning against obedience with a cause in Proverbs 16:2: "All a person's ways seem pure to them, but motives are weighed by the LORD." The Cleavers weren't fooled by Eddie Haskell, and God is not fooled by us. Yes, it is honorable to do the right thing. But doing the right things should be based on the overflow of our love from God, not to impress others or to get what we want.

Finally, we adjust our *want to* by avoiding obedience with a clause. A clause is a section of a contract that is used as a bargaining agreement between two parties. When writing a legal document, it is often necessary to include a clause or stipulation to protect the interests of both parties. A clause isn't necessary or advised when we respond to God. Yet many times, when things get tough and we need God to take immediate action, we often default to bargaining with Him. *God, if You* [insert clause], *then I will* [insert clause].

Bargaining with God is not necessary. God loves us and longs to shower us with the best gifts. We can be confident that He is always looking out for our best interests. Paul told us this: "And we know that in all things God works for the good of those who love him, who have been called according to his purpose" (Rom. 8:28). God is working for our good, and He deserves a committed yes rather than a clause-based yes.

This verse is such a comforting assurance from God, but what's kind of ironic is that it comes with a clause. Can you find it?

"In all things God works for the good of those [clause] *who love Him*." God's allowed to give us stipulations, and this one is important. The clause is for us to love God and to do His will. We demonstrate our love for Him through our obedience to Him. Jesus's words in John 14:15 are another very clear example of this kind of clause: "If you love me, keep my commands." Just as parents expect their children to obey them, God expects us to obey Him.

The life you've always wanted begins with yes to God.

Let's pause for a minute and think about John 14:15 differently. What if Jesus had declared the words in this way: "If you don't obey Me, then you don't love Me"? Yeah, I know. Stings a little bit, doesn't it? Essentially, each time we don't obey, or when we bargain for His blessings, we tell Him, "I really don't love You enough to say yes." Do those words pierce your heart as deeply as they pierce mine?

The obstacle of self is defeated when we believe God is always working for our good and when we confidently offer Him continued yeses without a pause, cause, or clause. Oh, friend, the life you've always wanted—one filled with peace in midst of trouble, love when you're told you're unlovable, affirmation in the face of rejection, and hope when optimism remains at bay—that life begins with yes to God.

Obedience cultivates trust. This trust will lead to abundant living (John 10:10) and can often involve adversity. As we study Paul, we will see he faced misfortune: from rejection to public floggings, to imprisonment, and to being shipwrecked. His life after his Damascus road experience was less than ideal, yet his *want to* never wavered.

FINDING MY WILLPOWER: THE OBSTACLE OF SIN

Sin is a huge obstacle to our pursuit of continual yeses and the immeasurably more life. Some days I wish God would just *make* me obey so I wouldn't sin. But what kind of relationship would that be? If this wish came true, we would never

- experience the mystery of His profound power, because we would never be weak.
- grip the intensity of His enduring love, because our actions would be robotic in nature.
- know the nearness of His presence, because we would never be in need.
- grasp the generosity of His grace, because we would never need forgiveness.

If we were to miss these attributes of God, we would miss the very essence of who He is. It is through our struggles that we get to know the heart of God, His love for us, and the depth of His faithfulness. It is through our hardships that we discover God's power that works in us to do His will (see Phil. 2:13).

With a God as faithful as our God, it's hard to fathom that we can be unfaithful to Him. Sin makes our willpower wane and our spirit weak. Even when we obey without a pause, cause, or clause, our heart is vulnerable to the seduction of sin, temptation. This must be dealt with on a daily basis.

Before we tackle this obstacle and the effect it has on our obedience, it's important to review some facts about sin to ensure we are all on the same page.

Fact 1: Sin was not part of God's plan. Adam and Eve introduced it into the world in the Garden of Eden (see Gen. 3:6). The sin nature was passed through the seed of Adam; therefore, we are born with a sin nature and don't have a say in the matter. As heirs to Adam, our inheritance is death, because the penalty for sin is death; however, Jesus satisfied our sin debt so that we could have eternal life. "When Adam sinned, sin entered the world. Adam's sin brought death, so death spread to everyone, for everyone sinned" (Rom. 5:12 NLT).

Fact 2: Sin separates us from God. "But your iniquities have separated you from your God; your sins have hidden his face from you, so that he will not hear" (Isa. 59:2). At first glance, this verse seems like horrible news, yet there's good news! We don't have to stay separated from God. He is faithful and just to forgive us, if we will humble ourselves and confess our sin (see 1 John 1:9).

Fact 3: Sin is forgiven and righteousness (being right with God) is possible because of Jesus. "Yes, Adam's one sin brings condemnation for everyone, but Christ's one act of righteousness brings a right relationship with God and new life for everyone" (Rom. 5:18 NLT). Praise God for Jesus! Praise Jesus for His sacrifice!

Fact 4: Sin remains a part of our life. Jesus's death removed the penalty and power of sin, but not its pull (temptation). "For sin will not rule over you, because you are not under law but under grace" (Rom. 6:14 HCSB). We have the Holy Spirit to help us resist sin, yet we often give way to the pull of the sin rather than rely on the power of the Spirit. The struggle will be real until Jesus returns and the presence of sin is eradicated forever.

Fact 5: Sin is not a disqualifier for the immeasurably more life; it is, however, a disrupter. The only way to be disqualified from the immeasurably more life is to reject God's invitation to be part of the life. "For 'Everyone who calls on the name of the LORD will be saved'" (Rom. 10:13 NLT).

Jesus's death removed the penalty and power of sin, but not its pull. As followers of Christ, we often don't want to admit that we sin. We like to diminish and soften our sin by using words like *mistake, error, judgment*, and *transgression*. By using muted words like these, we lessen the magnitude of Calvary. Christ obeyed His Father and accepted a cruel death on a cross so you and I could have the hope of living eternally with Him in heaven. John Piper once said that the first step to genuine spiritual health is to recognize your own sinfulness. No one wants to sign up for the "Yes, I'm a sinner and would love to tell you about my sins" class. But confessing sin to God and maintaining honest relationships with others preserve our relationship with God. Genuine spiritual health keeps our communication with God open and the obstacle of sin at bay.

I remember the day like it was yesterday. And while I don't recall the specific topic of the lesson, I have vividly retained the impact it had on me. Our chairs were in a circle, and I could hardly keep eye contact with the class members or our teacher. I'd been in Sunday school all my life, but I had never felt this before. My response to the lesson was shame, regret, sorrow, and complete humiliation. It hit me. It hit me hard. Twenty-plus years after my salvation experience, the weight of my sinfulness had finally hit me like a Mack truck going sixty-five miles per hour down the interstate: I was a sinner.

Somehow, I had managed to live as a Christian for two decades and never fully realized the greatness of my sin. Through seasons of sin and times of giving in to temptation, I had repented because I knew my sin was wrong. But I had never truly felt that weight or experienced grief over my sin.

This day was different. The pith of my sin fell on me like waves crashing against a retaining wall. How could the impact of my sin only now be realized after years of note taking, Bible verse highlighting, solo singing, and Bible study? Was my salvation experience real? Was I even saved?

I could not wait to get home from church, feed my people, and get them tucked in for naps. I rushed upstairs and collapsed in my Jesus chair to wrestle with my spirit for answers to my questions. This chair is where I had spent countless hours praying. It's where God had heard my complaints and responded to my questions. I received His love, wisdom, and understanding, but at this moment, like water from a fire hose, the memory of my sin began to flood my soul. The pain was overwhelming. Strangely enough, though, amid the pain, I felt freedom. The forgiveness He'd already given fell fresh on me. Yes, my salvation experience was real. Yes, I was saved. The Lord allowed me to experience the pain so I could have a small sense of the pain He had endured for me.

Jesus died so we could live in freedom from sin's power. He sent the Holy Spirit to see us through temptations and to resist their lure. Until Jesus returns, humans will always struggle with a wrestling match between flesh and spirit (old nature versus new nature). We will still sin, and even enjoy it, but guilt and conviction make sure we don't enjoy for it long. Paul spoke of this combat: "And I know that nothing good lives in me, that is, in my sinful nature. I want to do what is right, but I can't. I want to do what is good, but I don't. I don't want to do what is wrong, but I do it anyway" (Rom. 7:18–19 NLT). These verses don't feel very hopeful, do they? I mean, if Paul couldn't tame his old nature, what hope do we have of taming ours? Are we just doomed? There is good news: we are not doomed, because God has given us Himself—the Holy Spirit—to break free from old habits and sinful patterns.

We simply can't afford to do life apart from God.

The Holy Spirit is our reminder, our conviction, and our guide. "And He, when He comes, will convict the world concerning sin and righteousness and judgment" (John 16:8 NASB). He convicts; He does not condemn. His job is to produce godly sorrow within us that leads to repentance of our sin. God is omniscient, which means He already knows our sinful thoughts, emotions, and actions, yet He asks us to confess them to Him so we can be cleansed and receive His forgiveness.

How do we do this? One way is to have a "sin conversation" with the Holy Spirit each day—ask Him to bring to mind any ungodliness in your life and then seek His forgiveness and ask for His help to never return to your old ways. Because sin separates us from God, leaving it unchecked creates space between us and our heavenly Father. If our relationship is partitioned by sin, we aren't able to hear Him speak to us through His Word; and if we can't hear Him, we can't say yes to His instructions. We simply can't afford to do life apart from God.

Many years ago, I started praying a simple prayer written by King David. David, despite his sins of murder and adultery, was "a man after God's own heart" (see Acts 13:22). He was given this exalted description by God because he did all God asked him to do. I reasoned that if this was David's prayer, and he had found favor with God, perhaps I should pray it also. Maybe you can use this as a starting point in your sin conversation with God. Talking about sin isn't fun, but it is freeing. When you confess your sin, you will hurdle the sin obstacle and embrace the liberty to confidently continue to say yes to God.

> Search me [thoroughly], O God, and know my heart;
> Test me and know my anxious thoughts;
>
> And see if there is any wicked or hurtful way in me,
> And lead me in the everlasting way. (Ps. 139:23–24 AMP)

Keeping sin in check builds spiritual confidence. When we know we are right with God, our willpower to offer continual yeses grows stronger and our desire to please God intensifies. In a perfect world, we stay right with God, continue to live to please Him, and live in the immeasurably more experience; yet we don't live in a perfect world. We have an enemy who schemes against us with one obstruction after another. If he can't trip us with self, or kill our willpower, he will attempt to shame us into surrendering our worth.

Keeping sin in check builds spiritual confidence.

FINDING MY WORTH: THE OBSTACLE OF SHAME

Griffin had to be about four years old at the time. My little blond bundle of energy was just like every other child on the planet; he always wanted something new when we were out running errands. And like every other mother on the planet, I resisted as long as I could; but finally I would cave and agree to stop at one of the dollar-something-or-another stores. On one particular occasion I remember Griffin nearly bouncing to the toy aisle with excitement. He thoroughly surveyed the selections and carefully chose a superhero mask. That was the last time my little boy was simply Griffin for the next few months. He'd morph into a superhero by donning his mask whenever we weren't at preschool, church, or a doctor's appointment.

I'll be honest, with two kids and tons of toys, I didn't notice Griffin had stopped being a masked protector until the day I was cleaning behind the couch.

I'd proclaimed that our home needed to have *that* kind of cleaning day. You know—the day furniture gets moved, all the toys are removed from the shelves, and DVDs are returned to their proper cases. As each family member vigorously did their assigned tasks, I dragged the couch away from the wall to vacuum. Imagine my shock when I discovered the coveted mask tucked underneath the back flap, broken. I felt less than sympathetic. The mask my son had begged me to buy lay broken and hidden.

In my not-so-nice mommy voice, I questioned Griffin about why he'd hidden the mask. He didn't have any sound answers except for one: "I didn't want you to be mad at me." After some time in his room (no worries, I left some cleaning for him), we talked. I explained to Griffin that it's always best to tell the truth rather than hide the wrong he'd done, and I assured him that he would always be forgiven and loved. His four-year-old response was typical, "Okay, Mommy," then he ran off to finish his cleaning so he could play.

The accusing memory of our past sin is the enemy's tactic to keep the immeasurably more life just out of our reach.

He's seventeen now, and I recently asked him if he still felt bad about the broken mask. Griffin told me that he hadn't given that mask much thought over the last thirteen years. And before sharing this story with you, I hadn't either.

I know this is a story about a little boy and his toy, but we can draw a spiritual parallel from the forgotten mask to our forgiven sin and the weight of shame. Griffin felt shame and sorrow, so he hid the mask without telling me. I forgave him for breaking it and keeping the destruction a secret from me. Griffin accepted my forgiveness and moved beyond the incident. He did not allow the memory of his sin to haunt him or keep him from enjoying the future blessings of being my child.

The accusing memory of our past sin is the enemy's tactic to keep the immeasurably more life just out of our reach. Holding on to forgiven sin prevents us from receiving future blessings. To grasp the life Jesus died to give us, we have to open our hands and our heart to release our past. I love the way Paul said it:

> I do not mean that I am already as God wants me to be. I have not yet reached that goal, but I continue trying to reach it and to make it mine. Christ wants me to do that, which is the reason he made me his. Brothers and sisters, I know that I have not yet reached that goal, but there is one thing I always do. Forgetting the past and straining toward what is ahead, I keep trying to reach the goal and get the prize for which God called me through Christ to the life above. (Phil. 3:12–14 NCV)

Our goal is the same as Paul's—to become all that Christ created us to be and to accomplish the work He set before us. The obstacle of shame stands in the way of that goal. It's impossible to reach for something new when you're holding on to something old. The weight of shame is heavy, and we weren't created to lug it around our whole life. When we encountered Christ on our Damascus road, we became a new creation; we were pardoned from our past.

What I am about to share with you is revolutionary! If you are willing to receive this news, you will be changed forever. The words aren't mine; they belong to our friend Paul. I don't know if you underline, write, or highlight in your book, but you might want to grab a pen.

> So now there is no condemnation for those who belong to Christ Jesus. And because you belong to him, the

power of the life-giving Spirit has freed you from the power of sin that leads to death. (Rom. 8:1–2 NLT)

Oh, I wish I was right beside you. Did you catch it? We are not condemned! We belong to Christ! We are free! Indulge me for a minute while I get a bit bossy. Please highlight or underline the phrase *no condemnation for those who belong to Christ Jesus.* Circle the words *has freed.* Now pause and read this out loud, telling Satan: "Satan, I belong to Christ. I will no longer live a life of condemnation. Today I am owning the truth of Philippians 3:12–14 and Romans 8:1–2. You have to leave my mind, my presence, and my future. I am commanding you, with the life-giving power that God gave me, to flee and never return."

When we encountered Christ on our Damascus road, we became a new creation; we were pardoned from our past.

Shout hallelujah! This is a huge moment for you. Never forget you have the power of Christ in you and can send Satan packing. Beware, though, because he is a relentless rascal. Even though you kick him to the curb, he will always attempt to return to the scene of the crime (that is, he will try to tempt you in your weakness). Keep in mind that he is not omniscient (all knowing), but he does know our patterns and will return to the places where he's had past successes. His game is condemnation. God's way is conviction. Condemnation looks down because it is from Satan, whose purpose is to make us live in hopelessness. Conviction we welcome and looks up because it is from the Spirit, whose purpose is to help us live in holiness. It's imperative we understand the difference so we can recognize the deceiver when he attempts to stop us again with obstacles of shame and accusing memories.

Condemnation	Conviction
Looks down in remembering	Looks up and rejoices
Looks down in regret	Looks up with relief
Looks down in guilt	Look up in gratitude
Looks down in despair	Looks up with hope
Looks forward with doubt	Looks forward with optimism

Just as I forgave Griffin and forgot about the deception of the broken mask, God forgives and casts our sin away. In a song of praise, David wrote of God's handling of our sin: "As far as the east is from the west, so far has he removed our transgressions from us" (Ps. 103:12). God is omniscient; therefore, it is impossible for Him to forget anything. But don't be alarmed. The word *removed* tells us that God doesn't hold our sin against us once we are forgiven. What a comforting thought! He is such a gracious and merciful God.

> *Obedience aligns our heart with God's and opens the door for Him to become our magnificent obsession.*

It's okay to be honest—the struggle is real. Obedience isn't always easy. However, we can be confident that even in our obedience struggle, God is on our side. He is working in us, enabling us to desire and work out His good purpose (see Phil. 2:13).

This just blows my mind! Can you believe it? God works in us so that we desire to live according to His purpose. What an awesome

God! He enables us to do that which He calls us to do, even when we struggle. As we study Paul's life, we will see that he struggled as well, but he never waned in his *want to*, he discovered his *willpower* was Christ living in Him, and he knew his *worth* was defined at Calvary, not by his past. Obedience aligns our heart with God's and opens the door for Him to become our magnificent obsession.

ASK AND IMAGINE

Turn to chapter 10. With which obstacle do you most struggle? Finding your *want to*: the obstacle of self? Finding your willpower: the obstacle of sin? Or finding your worth: the obstacle of shame? What part of your life is affected most by this struggle? Moving forward, how will you overcome this obstacle?

3

Obsession of Yes

As I mentioned, I'm a bit of a word nerd. This realization makes me chuckle, because in school I had to work really hard to be a C student. Maybe you can relate. For God to choose me to author books and write Bible studies demonstrates that He is still in the miracle business and has a sense of humor. I've spent years looking up and studying words, and now I am a lover of words (and the Word, but more on that later). As we begin chapter 3, I feel it is important that we get a good understanding of the word *obsession*.

We're all probably familiar with this word. There have been books, movies, and songs written around it, but when was the last time you went to the dictionary to discover its meaning? The breakdown of the definition is fascinating and might even excite the word nerd in you. And it is really fun to read the definitions of words through spiritual lenses. So, for just a moment, pretend you are in English class and look at this word's root definition, as summarized from Dictionary.com:

Obsess: to think about something unceasingly or
persistently; dwell obsessively upon something; to
dominate or preoccupy the thoughts, feelings, or
desires of a person.[1]

Now, with a working definition, we can dig in. I'm curious, what is
your first thought when you hear the word *obsession*? My mind travels
back to my twenty-first birthday and the bottle of perfume Scott gave
me, Obsession by Calvin Klein. During different stages of my life, I've
been obsessed with a variety of desires and responsibilities. I remember
being boy crazy, label conscious, and hair aware. After I reached adulthood, I consistently dwelled on being successful in my job and having
the "perfect marriage." As a parent, my children's success, wellness, and
behavior dominated my thoughts and dictated my actions. For many
years, I was preoccupied with making things look perfect from the outside in an effort to make things on the inside better.

Our world sets us up for failure, but we don't see it because we
are busy following its suggestions for happiness. Power, position, and
possessions equal success. To measure up with what we perceive others
have, we are consumed by chasing the deal, making the next sale, or
getting the higher degree.

But our jobs, houses, cars, and bank accounts aren't the only things
we can be obsessed with. We often become consumed with our health
and happiness. The medical field reports good health is on the decline,
so we become absorbed with fitness. In order to reduce the stress in our
life, we take up a hobby only to find that reading, gardening, and home
decorating exhaust rather than relax us. Social media. Shopping. Politics.
Physical beauty. Don't mistake what I'm saying; an awareness of these

things isn't wrong. However, an awareness can turn into an obsession and quickly supersede our relationship with Christ. Goals and achievements are good; stewarding our bodies, money, and time is right. But these things shouldn't steal our focus from what really matters—that which will have eternal significance.

- Rather than asking, "Are my children successful?" ask "Are my children saved?"
- Rather than wondering, "How fast can I run a 10K?" ask "How quickly do I respond to the needs of others?"
- Rather than boasting, "My garden produced so much food," ask "With whom can I share my bounty?"

Being obsessed with the lesser things of life rather than focusing on eternity leaves little room for living with the God of immeasurably more.

Our world sets us up for failure, but we don't see it because we are busy following its suggestions for happiness.

For years, I was caught in the hamster wheel of the world. Do this. Look like this. One of my fixations was home improvement. HGTV was a huge influence on my life. All the do-it-yourself projects made me believe I actually could do it myself. My kitchen was painted five different colors in fifteen years, including one horrible experience with a faux painting technique called ragging. Each room in our home was given a facelift every three years or so. *If only my house could look like those on TV and in the magazines, there would be peace here and everything would be okay.* Perhaps, tucked somewhere in the back of my mind, I thought a prettier home would make a happier home, one Scott would feel better about. What I didn't realize at the time was that Scott's life-changing words had nothing to do with the external, but everything to do with the internal—my internal.

Obsessing about the external rather than focusing on the internal, leads to disappointment every time—a lesson that took me too long to learn. Anything that we obsess over that takes the place of God is an idol. I grieve over the years lost to fleshly living instead of God obsessing. You see, the immeasurably more life finds success in obsessing over the things of the Spirit, not of the flesh. "For those who live according to the flesh set their minds on the things of the flesh, but those who live according to the Spirit set their minds on the things of the Spirit" (Rom. 8:5 ESV). You and I are going to identify the things of the Spirit and how to make much of the them.

> **Being obsessed with the lesser things of life rather**
> **than focusing on eternity leaves little room for**
> **living with the God of immeasurably more.**

In his chart-topping hit "Magnificent Obsession," Steven Curtis Chapman sang: "Cut through these chains that tie me down to so many lesser things … Be my magnificent obsession."[2] As much as I hate to admit it, I still become overly occupied with the lesser things of this world. But I only have one obsession: His name is Jesus. Oh, dear one, I want to whisper something to your heart, so lean in closely: Determine to do the work necessary for Him to become your magnificent obsession. Make obedience paramount, conquer your obstacles, and obsess over the spiritual. He is worth it! The immeasurably more life is but one obsession away.

TRANSFORMING OUR OBSESSION

The first time I heard "Magnificent Obsession," I was moved to tears. Even after all these years, the lyrics still stir my heart as they did back then. I know why they tug on my heart now, but my younger self didn't fully grasp the answer. (These were the days my mind was reeling with the thirteen life-changing words.) Was I envious to sing the same song with my whole heart? Could I have been moved because I didn't know how to make God my magnificent obsession? Did the song's theme challenge me? Yes, yes, and yes. Little did I know, God well knew my heart and had set His providential plan in motion to transform my obsessions.

> *Determine to do the work necessary for Him to become your magnificent obsession. Make obedience paramount, conquer your obstacles, and obsess over the spiritual. He is worth it!*

Mind you, at this point in my adventure with God, I didn't know anything about transformation. The idea of obsessing over the wrong things never occurred to me. An immeasurably more life? What was that? Simply put, I was a hot-mess Christian who had been in church my entire life yet didn't know the basics of a Christian's transformation. I didn't know how to study the Bible, pray, or put action to my faith.

If you are feeling a little "woe is me" and experiencing a "me too" moment, pull up a chair. Make yourself at home. Let's talk, God-girl to God-girl.

Paul revealed the secret to transformation in his letter to the Romans. He heard that Christians were being undermined by a group trying to convince them that salvation was not through faith alone but also through the law. His letter to the church in Rome reminded them of the value of the law, and it encouraged them not to be confused by the naysayers. The law had its place, but it had nothing to do with salvation. Salvation comes through Christ alone. In Romans 12, Paul taught Christians how to keep their minds focused on what is godly rather than become influenced by the world around them. What a timely truth for all generations for all times! "Don't copy the behavior and customs of this world, but let God transform you into a new person by changing the way you think. Then you will learn to know God's will for you, which is good and pleasing and perfect" (Rom. 12:2 NLT).

Dictionary.com says that transformation is a "change in form, appearance, nature, or character."[3] Change is not popular in our culture; it's even less popular with me. The older I get, the more stubborn and set in my ways I become. But if transformation helps me know and be more like God, then sign me up!

I'll be the first to admit, some of Paul's writings can be challenging and may take a couple of readings to completely grasp his message. However, his wisdom and teaching have helped me grow my obsession with God. *Me.* For example, brother Paul gives us a practical, two-step instructional plan to revolutionize our relationship with God. (I'm a simple girl who loves a simple plan. Thanks, Paul!)

Instruction 1: Don't copy what the world is doing. We can't get comfy with the ways of this world and live as if this is all there is to life.

What does the word *home* bring to mind for you? For many, it's a place to kick off their shoes, relax on the couch, relish comfort food, and let their guard down. These things are great, but it's not okay to do this with the ways of this world. We can't get comfortable with gossip, gluttony, pornography, workaholism, affairs, and a myriad of other sins. This world is not our home. "But our citizenship is in heaven, and from it we await a Savior, the Lord Jesus Christ" (Phil. 3:20 ESV). Therefore, doesn't it make more sense to become like our heavenly Father in our heavenly home?

The world says	**God says**
Serve yourself.	"For even the Son of man came not to be served but to serve" (Mark 10:45 ESV).
Put your needs first.	"The last will be first, and the first last" (Matt. 20:16 ESV).
Amass possessions.	"But store up for yourselves treasures in heaven" (Matt. 6:20).
Purity doesn't matter.	"Flee from sexual immorality" (1 Cor. 6:18 ESV).
Get your name out there.	"Our Father in heaven, hallowed be your name" (Matt. 6:9 ESV).
Even the score.	"Bear with each other and forgive one another" (Col. 3:13).
Use others.	"Be kind to one another, tenderhearted" (Eph. 4:32 ESV).
Work for your own gain.	"Whatever you do, whether in word or deed, do it all in the name of the Lord Jesus" (Col. 3:17).

*We can't get comfy with the ways of this world
and live as if this is all there is to life.*

Doesn't transforming to be like Christ look easy when God's words are simply listed? In the days of Paul, the Pharisees (the world) laid many man-made rules on God's people. This oppression caused them to be stressed out, and this is why they needed Jesus. Today, with our television shows, movies, and social media all pouring sex, violence, retaliation, self-advancement, and get-it-while-you-can thinking down our throat, imitating Christ can feel like swimming against the current rather than an easy list to check off. We can get worn out and grow tired of doing the right thing when it doesn't seem to be making a difference. We need Jesus and the easy rhythm of His grace. Be encouraged with this verse: "So let's not get tired of doing what is good. At just the right time we will reap a harvest of blessing if we don't give up" (Gal. 6:9 NLT).

And when it gets really bad, and the current keeps taking us down, we can turn to these words:

> Are you tired? Worn out? Burned out on religion? Come to me. Get away with me and you'll recover your life. I'll show you how to take a real rest. Walk with me and work with me—watch how I do it. Learn the unforced rhythms of grace. I won't lay anything heavy or ill-fitting on you. Keep company with me and you'll learn to live freely and lightly. (Matt. 11:28–30 THE MESSAGE)

Isn't God so sweet to encourage our hearts with His awesome Word? I just can't live without it! But sometimes He can also encourage us without our ever opening the Bible.

I used to go to church with a man who, from what I could tell, seemed to have mastered many items on the "God says" side of the list. From what I knew of him, he never appeared to be drowning in the current of the world. He always smiled and had kind things to say to everyone. I knew I liked him from the first hello, and when I discovered who he really was, I liked him even more.

Every Sunday morning, my husband and I would usher our children to their respective classes before going to our Sunday school group. An hour later we'd collect our kids and head to the main sanctuary to sit in our regular balcony pew for the worship service. Each week I'd notice the little yellow pencils, sharpened with perfect points, tucked into the back of the pew in front of us to use for taking notes.

I never thought much about the perfectly sharpened pencils until I happened to be at the church office one morning. A dapper, older gentleman brushed by with a box of pencils in one hand and a sharpener in the other. With a bent brow, I asked someone, "Is he the one who sharpens the pew pencils each week?" My guess was confirmed.

Before the next church service, this man would quietly and faithfully serve our congregation with few taking notice of his act. And the beauty in it all? He didn't want anyone to notice. He didn't want recognition, a pat on the back, or even a thank-you. It was his simple way of serving the Lord and investing in eternity. When we serve in secret, God gives us the greatest fulfillment—the realization that serving others brings joy, and this joy pleases Jesus. The one who serves unnoticed is the one who loves God more than the praise of others.

Sharpening pencils for no recognition or pay is just one example of how *not to copy the world.* There are endless ways to be less like the world and more like Jesus—all of which, if we invest in them, will turn our eyes to God and increase our obsession with Him.

Become a regular volunteer in the food pantry in your community. Read a book or watch an educational program instead of crass, late-night shows. Donate the money you were going to spend on another pair of shoes to a relief organization that provides shoes to children in third-world countries. Bless someone by giving up the parking space closest to the door. Enable safety features on your computer that block sites of a sexual nature. Use funds set aside for a movie to purchase a gift card for a single mother.

> **The one who serves unnoticed is the one who**
> **loves God more than the praise of others.**

The line between living like the world and living in agreement with the ways of God may seem a bit blurry and unnatural at first. However, as we learn to follow Paul's first instruction, the pull to live like the world, and our obsession with the lesser things, will fade.

Intermission: We interrupt this chapter for a brief intermission to share some extremely important information.

We've talked about the word *spiritual* in different contexts over the last few chapters. As we get ready to dive into Paul's second instruction, it'll be helpful for us to be on the same page regarding the concept of spiritual things. So, let's park here for a minute. Thinking through this will lay a great foundation for instruction 2.

The Holy Spirit has been spoken of several times already. Maybe in your reading you've wondered, *Who exactly is the Holy Spirit? Where did He come from? Where does He live?* These are great questions. If you already know, hang tight with me—a refresher never hurt anyone, right?

The Holy Spirit is the third person in what Christians refer to as the Trinity—the three persons of God: God the Father, God the Son (Jesus), and God the Spirit. No one fully grasps this mystery of three persons in one, but we can know some things about the Holy Spirit from what Scripture tells us. The Holy Spirit is a thinking and knowing person (1 Cor. 2:10). God's Holy Spirit can feel sorrow (Eph. 4:30). The Spirit pleads to God on our behalf (Rom. 8:26–27). The Spirit gives us gifts and makes decisions about them (1 Cor. 12:7–11).

The Spirit renews us when we accept Christ as our Savior so that we can participate in the divine nature of God.

In the Old Testament, the Holy Spirit *roamed*, empowering certain people for service to and communication with God. "For the eyes of the LORD range throughout the earth to strengthen those whose hearts are fully committed to him" (2 Chron. 16:9). However, in the New Testament, the Holy Spirit *resided* in believers. "Do you not know that your bodies are temples of the Holy Spirit, who is in you, whom you have received from God? You are not your own" (1 Cor. 6:19). The Spirit is a gift from God Himself to help, guide, remind, and teach us

His ways (see John 14:26). The Spirit renews us when we accept Christ as our Savior (see Titus 3:5) so that we can participate in the divine nature of God (see 2 Pet. 1:4).

Spiritual things pertain to our spiritual life: God's Word, prayer, worship, and service. The Holy Spirit aids our understanding of God's Word (see 1 John 2:27), communicates to the Father for us in prayer (see Rom. 8:26–27), and enables us to worship in spirit and truth (see John 4:23–24); and the overflow of His love compels us to serve others. The flesh can't manufacture such things; only the Spirit can generate spiritual things. They proceed, come from, or are sent by the Holy Spirit to connect us with God. God's Word, prayer, worship, and service *apart* from the indwelling of the Holy Spirit have no meaning in the life of the believer. This is why the biggest and first yes (salvation) is so important. Without the Holy Spirit, we cannot live with the God of immeasurably more.

End Intermission

Instruction 2: Let God transform the way you think. Paul's first instruction focuses on turning away from worldly things. The next phase of the practical, two-step instructional plan to revolutionize our relationship with God focuses on turning our minds toward spiritual things.

When Paul met Jesus on the Damascus road, he had the knowledge of the Word (at this time only the Old Testament had been recorded) but not the power of the Spirit. His parents were wealthy Pharisees and middle-class leaders in the community. The Pharisees accepted the written Word of God but held it equal to the rituals and traditions of the Old Testament and the law of Moses. This sect of Jews read, studied, and followed the Old Testament and its laws. However, they took the law beyond what God had intended by adding hundreds of extra rules that became their traditions. Over the years, these people treated their traditions as equal to God's written Word and strictly adhered to both. As Deuteronomy 4:2 reminds us, though, this is a huge no-no: "You shall not add to the word that I command you, nor take from it, that you may keep the commandments of the LORD your God that I command you" (ESV).

The Pharisees adhered to the strict letter of the Jewish law. When Paul turned thirteen, his parents sent him to learn under a well-known Pharisee, Rabbi Gamaliel. This highly respected and influential teacher schooled Paul for the next six years. Under Gamaliel's tutelage, Paul learned to be as committed to his Jewish faith as he was to Old Testament and Pharisaical laws.

I love knowing all this about Paul. He is living proof that God can use our past to prepare us for our future. Paul's investment in the Scriptures didn't go to waste. He spent the latter part of his life on mission trips establishing churches and mentoring disciples. All the years of studying the law had prepared Paul to speak to those who thought they had to adhere to the law to be saved. And through his salvation experience, Paul clearly realized that the law he had studied didn't save; only faith in Jesus could.

Without the Holy Spirit, we cannot live with the God of immeasurably more.

The transforming of the mind is twofold. We must have both the Holy Spirit and the Word, the Bible. We've already talked about the

Spirit. Now we will unlock the other component of instruction 2: transforming our minds. Paul set the example for us. It's up to us to put in the time to learn the Word.

BEING MORE THAN A CARRIER

In recognition of my decision to follow Christ, my parents gave me a copy of *The Children's Living Bible.* Oh, how I wish I could show it to you. My mother completed the dedication page in her elegant cursive handwriting. The name of the Bible is embossed in gold lettering on the green spine. The cover has a beautiful watercolor picture of Jesus holding a small sheep on His shoulders. I felt so grown-up carrying that Bible to church.

I loved that Bible for no other reason than that it was God's Word. Over the years I have gotten new Bibles of varying translations with different study features. I've always held the Bible in high esteem. It's been a constant companion in the passenger seat of my car. His Word has traveled with me to the beach and to the mountains on family vacations.

In the desperate days following that hard conversation with Scott, I realized all my carrying had been in vain. When I needed help the most from Scripture, I didn't know how to find it. Here's the crazy thing— I had been praying and reading the Bible on a daily basis. Chapters and verses glowed in highlighter yellow. Notes filled the margins, and colored lines marked important scriptures. My Bible study blanks were filled in. But the hard reality hit me: I was only a carrier of God's Word. I was the exact opposite of Paul. I had the Spirit without the Word.

I approached God with the simple prayer, *Help me.* I was so embarrassed. How could I have been in church, invested so much time in Bible study, yet still not really known how to hear His Word? My upbringing couldn't have been better. Church leaders had taught me about the Bible, helped me memorize Scripture, and even shown me how to have quiet time. But because I didn't put in the work to know the Word, I didn't know the Word. Finally, after twenty years, I came to a place where I wanted to actually understand the words I'd memorized, underlined, and heard preached. Here's how I started.

The bare-bone beginnings were a mix of me, a grown-up version of the Living Bible (*The One Year Chronological Bible*), and Jesus. I was determined to love God's Word because I knew it, not just because God wrote it. I seriously had no idea what I was doing.

I prayed another simple prayer, *All right, Lord. Let's do this thing.* The Bible translation I chose to begin my studies with was arranged in the chronological order of how the events transpired, and it was structured in bite-sized daily readings. It was fun and fresh as I read through the stories in Genesis that I had learned in church. Then I got to the middle of Exodus when God gave Moses the law. Like the snake he is, the enemy slithered in to remind me that I was only a C student and probably shouldn't continue since I wasn't smart enough to understand what I was reading. His reminder made me think. I went from being excited about reading the Bible to wanting to skip portions of it.

And what about all those laws, Lord? Exodus, Leviticus, Numbers, and Deuteronomy … those are supposed to be really hard to understand. I don't have to read those, do I, Lord? Since I'm under the new covenant of Jesus, I can skip to Matthew, right?

Have you asked the same questions? Have you avoided God's Word out of fear? Fear you wouldn't understand? Or maybe fear that you *would* understand?

Much to no one's surprise, I didn't sense the Holy Spirit say, *Sure, sweetie, just skip those parts of the Old Testament like they never happened.* In trepidation I continued, never really understanding or finding anything applicable to my life until I read, "The LORD our God has secrets known to no one. We are not accountable for them, but we and our children are accountable forever for all that he has revealed to us, so that we may obey all the terms of these instructions" (Deut. 29:29 NLT). Who would have thought that out of the 31,000-plus verses in the Bible, my favorite would be from a book I always avoided reading?

When Moses told the Israelites about the "secret things" of God, he was talking about that which God will likely never reveal to humans. So we must know from the very beginning of becoming *more than a carrier* that there are things we will never know, and we have to be at peace with not knowing. I can attest that, with what He does teach me through the inspiration of the Word and the Holy Spirit, what I don't know doesn't hold me captive. You see, whether we are an A student or an F student, we can freely read God's Word *without* fear of *not* understanding.

God reveals what He needs us to know on a need-to-know basis—when He feels we need to and are mature enough in our faith to know. "Ask me and I will tell you remarkable secrets you do not know about things to come" (Jer. 33:3 NLT). We can study Scripture in freedom rather than in fear. Since my Deuteronomy 29:29 revelation, I have a process for how I approach Scripture. Let me share it with you:

1. Read the passage of Scripture. I read the *One Year Chronological Bible: NLT* every day. The New Living Translation is one I can easily understand.

2. Pray for understanding and application. *Lord, reveal what You want me to know.*

3. Open my computer to read and study different commentaries on free sites: Studylight.org, Biblehub.com, and Biblegateway.com. Some of the celebrated Bible commentaries I recommend are from Matthew Henry, David Guzik, and Jamieson-Fausset-Brown.

4. Celebrate what the Spirit reveals and make notes in my journal of how I can live the truth out in my daily life. And if I still don't understand? I move on. Yes, I said I move on. I trust God to reveal what He wants me to know when He wants me to know it. It's important to live out what He reveals rather than get caught up in what we don't understand.

Here's the thing: the devil wants to keep us ignorant of the Word by trapping us in the insecurity of our intelligence. My disdain for him is rising as I write. He wants God's people to stay dead to the Word because he knows the Word is life: "Turn my eyes from worthless things, and give me life through your word" (Ps. 119:37 NLT). Paul says we must transform our minds, but not as the world does. God-girls do the opposite of the world. We transform our minds with the power of God's Word.

You see, whether we are an A student or an F student, we can freely read God's Word without fear of not understanding.

Learning how to read the Word is only part of the work necessary for God to become our obsession. The work of mind transformation really starts when we are challenged to *live* the Word. Philippians 2:4 comes to mind: "Do not merely look out for your own personal interests, but also for the interests of others" (NASB). Before learning and living the Word, I primarily cared about only the things that concerned me. Paul's words in this verse challenged me to the core, and my initial response was not one of my finer moments.

My friend Stacy had children between the ages of my daughter and son. As our kids outgrew their clothes, Stacy and I would swap hand-me-downs with each other. It always bothered her when she took clothes from me but didn't have any to give back, which was often the case. One day Stacy received two huge bags full of clothes a few sizes too big for her son. With sheer joy, she called me to come get the clothes, and with sheer joy I accepted.

When I picked up the clothes, the nosy person in me couldn't wait until I got home to see what treasures filled the bags. We opened the sacks and were amazed at the fine clothes, some new with tags. Most were sized just a little big for my Griffin, but I decided I'd save them until he grew into them. I loaded up my car and left with my bounty.

For some reason, I went home a different way than usual. Looking back now, I know why: God had an appointment for me. The fading light of the setting sun cast a soft glow on a family standing in their yard, blankly staring at the charred remains of their house. Fire had engulfed and destroyed everything. As I passed the house and noticed the young teenage boy in the yard, my mind flashed to the bags of clothes that Stacy had given me. Instantly, I knew what God's Word would have me do; however, I did not stop. I continued to drive and argue with God. *Those are for Griffin. They were given to us.* Conviction overwhelmed me to the point of obedience, however. And the large parking lot ahead provided the perfect place to turn around.

I'd reached a point in my obsession with God that I desired to live out His Word more than I longed to keep those clothes. I wanted to live out Scripture: "Do not merely look out for your own personal interests, but also for the interests of others."

Life with the God of immeasurably more is found at the intersection of His Word and our complete obedience to it.

These words came alive as I tried to communicate with the young man, who spoke broken English. *Jesus loves you. He asked me to give you these clothes.* The young man retrieved the bags from the back of my van and in his language told his mother what I said. But that day I learned that Jesus and kindness don't need to be translated. They are understood in every language.

We have to be students of the Word, never suspending our learning. Life with the God of immeasurably more is found at the intersection of His Word and our complete obedience to it. We experience His power and His pleasure with our yeses. Learning the Word without living the Word is luminosity. Living the Word without loving the Word is legalism. Learning the Word leads to living the Word. When we really live it, in obedience to God, we will fall madly in love with it, as well as its amazing Author. This love brings about liberty.

THE LETTER SAYS IT ALL

My mom had barely entered her teenage years when my dad—seventeen at the time—saw her over the hood of the bus he drove and said, "Someday, I'm gonna marry that girl." He did marry her, and this year they celebrated sixty-four years of marriage. He has cherished her since the first time he laid eyes on her. I know because I've read his love notes.

My daddy was a carpenter by trade. As an early riser, he made it to the job site before daylight. Each morning, after he packed his peanut-butter-and-banana sandwich and filled his thermos with coffee, he wrote the same words on a torn piece of scrap paper: "I love you today." When my mother made her way to the kitchen to pour her coffee, she'd read his simple love letter. As one year faded into the next, their love remained strong, and my daddy continued to write my momma love notes.

Several years ago, my daddy's once-steady hands began to fail him. His doctor diagnosed him with familial tremors, a condition where shaking and small, rapid movements affect the arms, head, eyelids, and other muscles. People with this disorder have trouble holding and using small objects … and writing love notes.

My daddy had always been active. Even though he had slowed down some in his eighties, he still kept busy. Sadly, though, this disorder disrupted his life tremendously. As the condition worsened, he asked his doctor for some medicine, but not for reasons you would think. He wasn't concerned about his golf swing or holding a hammer. Instead, as he explained to his physician, "You see, I write her love notes each day, and now I can't."

My parents came to dinner at my house shortly after my dad started on the right medicine for his tremors. As I greeted my daddy at the door with a hug, he reached into his pocket and handed me a small, torn piece of scrap paper. Written were the words "I love you, Wendy Pope." His entire faced beamed. "See, I can write love notes again."

That note, a couple of years old now, hangs on the mirror in my bathroom. Every day as I apply my makeup and fix my hair, I read the love note from my father. I never have to wonder if he loves me, because his words say it all.

I don't know what your relationship with your earthly father is like, but I know a Father who loves you very much. He sent His Son to die a sacrificial death so that you could spend eternity with Him. He sent His Holy Spirit to dwell within you as a teacher, guide, comforter, and helper. Be obsessed with Him; He's obsessed with you. His Word says it all.

Before knowing Paul's instructional plan, I was only a carrier of God's Word—a woman who tried to carefully walk the tightrope between the world and my faith. Now, I am a lover of God's Word—a woman who runs the race of faith with liberty and joy. Paul's simple two-step plan certainly revolutionized my relationship with God, and it will do the same for your relationship with Him.

Be obsessed with Him; He's obsessed with you. His Word says it all.

The enemy will still attempt to entice you with the lesser things of this world. He's relentless like that. Occupy your mind with one obsession only: Jesus Christ. Allow the spiritual things to dominate your thoughts and feelings. Make obedience paramount, conquer your obstacles, and obsess over the spiritual. God is worth it! When He becomes our obsession, saying yes to Him and no to self becomes as natural as breathing.

ASK AND IMAGINE

Turn to chapter 10. What are some of your current obsessions? Paul's two-part instruction in Romans 12:2 is challenging. Instruction 1: Don't copy what the world is doing. How are you currently copying the world? Instruction 2: Let God transform the way you think. What adjustments can you make in your life to allow God to begin the transformation process in you?

Section Two

No Invites Revelation

I can do all things through Christ who strengthens me.

Philippians 4:13 NKJV

4

Note to Self: Accepting My New Image

I met Lauren—one of my daughter's middle school friends—early in my season of transformation. The two girls couldn't have been more different. Blaire is a realist, and Lauren is an optimist. On our carpool days Lauren walked to the car dressed as if she had just stepped off the fashion pages—matching from head to toe in the latest trend, makeup perfectly applied, and a purse full of girly things hanging on her shoulder. My Blaire? Beautiful for sure, but in her own way: jeans, T-shirt, low-top Converse, and hair pulled up that shouted, "I was asleep until five minutes ago." It has always shocked me that they found each other, but who can know how two girls become friends?

After all these years, I've discovered that God brought Lauren into Blaire's life because she needed a friend and I needed training. My relationship with Lauren was the genesis of my learning to say no to self, while gagging on the words.

*We're not in boot camp anymore. We are in combat
training—learning to say no to self in a self-first world.*

Offering God continual yeses is just the beginning of the immeasurably more life. If we stopped with yeses to God, we would miss
our personal transformation and the revelation of our real purpose: to
bring glory to Him by being a display of His splendor so that all people
will be drawn to God and be saved. Can you even believe we get to
be a part of someone else's salvation story? The story is not about us,
what God does for us, or what we can do for Him. It's all about God.
It's about us following His plan and making sure everyone knows Him
through a personal relationship with Jesus Christ. Saying yes to God
not only secures our place in eternity but invites the revelation of who
we are and who we are not—we are not God, not someone's salvation,
and not in charge. It's important that we grasp this sobering truth: we
are only a part of God's story because of His amazing grace.

I wouldn't be a friend if I didn't warn you: saying yes to God is
actually the easiest part of living with the God of immeasurably more.
The next three chapters are the toughest of this book. We're not in boot
camp anymore. We are in combat training—learning to say no to self
in a self-first world.

*In living no to self, we give God permission
to mess with our beautiful.*

Saying yes to God is like secret keeping with your best friend. You
spend time with Him—sharing your pain, dreams, hopes, and fears.
You laugh and cry together. He encourages you through the life-giving

truths of His Word. When He asks you to do something, you say yes, and the yes fills you with His pleasure.

Our salvation and intimacy with God are beautiful things, but they are only part of the immeasurably more life. Another key component is saying no to ourselves. In living no to self, we give God permission to mess with our beautiful. The trust relationship is strengthened as we live counterculturally to the world around us and embrace the life He died to give us.

I'm not trying to scare you into abandoning the journey. But it's important you know that the immeasurably more life doesn't come without cost. Ask Paul. He was beaten, flogged, rejected, and imprisoned. From prison he wrote, "Yes, everything else is worthless when compared with the infinite value of knowing Christ Jesus my Lord. For his sake I have discarded everything else, counting it all as garbage, so that I could gain Christ" (Phil. 3:8 NLT). Ask Jesus. He was betrayed, scorned, whipped, beaten, and crucified. His response: "Father, if you are willing, take this cup from me; yet not my will, but yours be done" (Luke 22:42).

Whatever you give up for the cause of Christ won't compare to the gain you'll receive in living the immeasurably more life.

Like Paul, countless numbers of Christians around the world and across the span of time have been condemned for their faith in Christ. They've endured brutalities and injustices that many of us will never suffer even a fraction of. There are Christians who have paid the ultimate price with their lives for living their faith out loud. But for the majority of Christ followers, the losses we will experience are our pride, maybe some relationships, possibly position, perhaps some possessions, and probably a few personal wants. Some of these things may be heartbreaking. Perhaps you've lost a lifelong friend because of your commitment to Christ. Maybe you left a job because your beliefs didn't align with company policy. While such experiences don't compare with being imprisoned, tortured, or murdered, they can be difficult to walk through, despite having peace from the Lord.

I can promise you this: whatever you give up for the cause of Christ won't compare to the gain you'll receive in living the immeasurably more life. When you arrive at the place where the things of this world are as refuse, it will take your breath away, and every sacrifice you made will be worth it. Oh, please hang in there with me and on to the commitment you made to study God's Word and to pursue an active prayer life. They are your sustaining power to say no to self.

PEELING BACK THE ONION

We left Lauren and my training back there somewhere, so let me pick up the story. I wasn't expecting a personal transformation when I volunteered to grab Lauren and her siblings from school for their mom. Since five kids were going to be at my house for lunch, I decided to pick up a couple of pizzas while running my errands earlier in the day: one cheese pizza for the kiddos and a pepperoni, ham, and pineapple pizza just for me. (Sometimes we just need a pizza only for us.)

When we got to my house, the kids unloaded their backpacks and got started on lunch while I unpacked the groceries from the van (and set *my* pizza away from *their* pizza). After I emptied the van and all the provisions were put away, I poured myself an ice-cold Dr Pepper. My mouth was watering for a slice of my favorite pie.

As I moved toward the box, I noticed the lid had been lifted. *Hmm? How'd that happen? Maybe one of the kids thought it was the cheese pizza.* Imagine my displeasure when I opened the box to find two slices missing. (Gasp!) *Who would dare touch my prized pizza?*

Then, out of my fog, a voice squealed in sheer delight, "Oh, Mrs. Pope, I love pepperoni, ham, and pineapple too."

With a jaw-clinching, sideways grin, I replied, "How fun! Nobody in my family likes it." I stood over the box eating what was left of my lunch like a security guard at the White House.

It gets worse.

After lunch, I sat down to prepare my Read Thru the Word Bible study lesson. My tummy was satisfied, and now my spirit would be too. The girls were in the kitchen as Blaire finished emptying the dishwasher. I have to admit; I love to listen to tween girls talk and giggle. I was half-listening and half-studying when I heard my name followed by a question, "Momma, do we have any chocolate?"

In an instant, I found myself caught in the horns of a dilemma and an inner debate. *I can tell the truth, or I can tell a lie.* You see, there was a bag of Ghirardelli Dark Chocolate Raspberry Squares in the kitchen cabinet. I hadn't bothered to hide them, because no one in my family likes Ghirardelli Dark Chocolate Raspberry Squares. (Don't judge me. You know you've hidden your favorite candy before.)

What is a good Christian woman who loves chocolate and Jesus supposed to do in a situation like that? Well, I'm sorry to disappoint you, but I didn't respond in the way a good Christian woman should have.

"I don't think we have any chocolate."

Yes, I most certainly did sit there with the Holy Scriptures in my lap and tell a lie.

The reply came back from my daughter. "What about the Ghirardelli Dark Chocolate Raspberry Squares?"

"No one likes those except me."

The response? "Lauren *loves* Ghirardelli Dark Chocolate Raspberry Squares."

Of course she does.

In a split second, the Holy Spirit pierced my heart with the conviction of my selfishness. I knew I had no other choice but to offer Lauren my stash of beloved, decadent treats.

The Spirit's conviction consumed my heart. Immediately I sensed God's disapproval. Sickened by my behavior, I asked God to forgive me. With my soul realigned with Him, I was able to proceed with my lesson preparation as a slightly transformed woman, who had just been schooled about how to be more like the Lord in truth and graciousness.

Lauren slept over that night. I have no idea what time those silly girls finally conked out, but they were sleeping like lambs when I woke up to have my quiet time with Jesus. After a sweet time studying God's Word, I was full of the Spirit when I tiptoed downstairs to fix my breakfast. I couldn't wait for a bite of a buttered English muffin and to taste the fresh, sweet strawberries I had bought the day before. With my muffin toasting, and my heart refreshed with Jesus, I opened the refrigerator to discover a half-empty container of strawberries. Then it hit me, *Lauren likes strawberries too.*

Living no to self invites God to get in our business—to peel back the onion. Just as an onion has many layers, we have many layers.

During this phase of our journey, God will begin to pull our layers back to reveal the *real* us. The real me I saw that day was ugly. She was a selfish, deceptive liar. Ouch! It hurts to describe myself with those harsh words, but the truth is the truth, and sometimes it hurts.

> *Our craving to know Christ has to be greater*
> *than our concern over our hurt feelings.*

In these moments of revelation, we are confronted with three choices: ignore it, choose condemnation, or respond with repentance. When we

- ignore the revelation, we tell God, "I'm not serious about being a Christian. Sundays are enough for me."
- choose condemnation, we tell Satan, "You were right. I'm not good enough to live a life of faith and experience the immeasurably more life."
- respond with repentance, we cry out to God, "I am a sinner. You are my Savior. Your grace is sufficient to cover my sins."

You might be asking, *Why would anyone want to see the ugly in themselves? Isn't life hard enough without exposing my sin?* So why should we face up to the ugly? Because God transforms ugly to lovely, and He brings wellness through pain. Remember, I was in a desperate place in my marriage and my life. God was my only option. Here's a hard fact of life: if we're not currently in a tough spot, we very well may be later down the road. As Jesus said in John 16:33, "In this world you will have trouble. But take heart! I have overcome the world."

> *We can't just accept all the positive things from*
> *God without accepting the polishing as well.*

That trouble is a promise. It's not *if*, but *when*. I don't say this to discourage you, but to encourage you that whether you are going through a difficult season now, today is the best time to seek God and to be transformed. The more you know Christ and become like Him, the better you'll be able to handle tough situations as His Word guides and tells us to. Our craving to know Christ has to be greater than our concern over our hurt feelings.

We can't just accept all the positive things from God without accepting the polishing as well. This transformation phase is hard, plain hard. It's why many people don't go beyond their first yes (salvation) to God—they neglect God's Word, prayer, and the church and local community. Sure, they may sit in their seat at church Sunday after Sunday, content with singing and hearing preaching once a week, but they stop short of the immeasurably more life and settle for mediocrity. When God gets too close, and things get uncomfortable, we turn tail and run. It isn't pleasant to see who we *really* are, but through God's grace, when the revelation comes, we are standing in the light of His love.

I want to share five sustaining truths that carried me through the peeling season. Highlight them. Write them on a piece of paper and keep them with your Bible. Read them each day during your time with God. Speaking truth to ourselves gives life.

> 1. *He loves me.* "But God is so rich in mercy, and he loved us so much, that even though we were dead because of our sins, he gave us life when he raised Christ from the dead" (Eph. 2:4–5 NLT).
>
> 2. *He is for me.* "If God is for us, who can be against us?" (Rom. 8:31).
>
> 3. *He is with me.* "This is my command—be strong and courageous! Do not be afraid or discouraged. For the LORD your God is with you wherever you go" (Josh. 1:9 NLT).
>
> 4. *His ways and thoughts are higher than mine.* "For just as the heavens are higher than the earth, so my ways are higher than your ways and my thoughts higher than your thoughts" (Isa. 55:9 NLT).
>
> 5. *I was made to be like Him.* "So God created human beings in his own image. In the image of God he created them; male and female he created them" (Gen. 1:27 NLT).

I can't stress enough the importance of the basics: daily time in His Word and an active prayer life. During my season of transformation, God and I had an early morning appointment every day. For over a year I prayed Psalm 139:23–24, giving Him permission to mess with me:

Search me [thoroughly], O God, and know my heart;
Test me and know my anxious thoughts;

And see if there is any wicked or hurtful way in me,
And lead me in the everlasting way. (AMP)

Without a foundation built on these spiritual basics, our flesh
will fail, and we'll always reflect ourselves instead of the Lord. The
immeasurably more life will forever remain an arm's length away.
Before Scott and I had *the* conversation, I wasn't thinking about living the immeasurably more life. My goal was to be a better version
of myself. It was in the peeling season that I needed a new image
consultant, because I looked nothing like who God had created me
to be.

Image Consulting

When I was young, I had several "image consultants." My feathered
hair was inspired by the *Charlie's Angels* star Farrah Fawcett. Gloria
Vanderbilt designed jeans perfect for me. The gold whipstitch and
swan logo on the right coin pocket made a great final touch to the
dark-wash pants. Izod Lacoste influenced the tops I sported. This
is how I rolled and who I modeled myself after in middle and high
school.

Even as I grew into adulthood and had my own family, I allowed
myself to be influenced by the world around me. Hindsight is 20/20.
I can now clearly see how I put my budget in jeopardy just so I could
be in fashion. Watching television shows that didn't define godly

lifestyles and decorating our home like the home improvement programs fed my desire to be accepted by the world. I wasn't familiar with the real meaning of Romans 12:2, "Do not conform to the pattern of this world, but be transformed by the renewing of your mind."

I'm not sure how entangled I would've become without the intervention of Scott's life-changing words. God heard my "Help me" cry and used the pain of Scott's words to show me the truth of the image I was reflecting—and it wasn't God's.

Not only did God create us, but He also continues to display His creative genius in our lives through the transforming work of the Holy Spirit.

I wasn't created in the image of Farrah, Gloria, Mr. Lacoste, or any other earthly mover, shaker, or trendsetter. "Then God said, 'Let us make mankind in our image, in our likeness.' So God created mankind in his own image, in the image of God he created them; male and female he created them" (Gen. 1:26–27). God, in conjunction with the Son and the Spirit, decided to fashion man in His likeness. Since women are from the seed of Adam, females are also created in the likeness of God. Dictionary.com tells us that the word *created* means "to cause to come into being, as something unique that would not naturally evolve or that is not made by ordinary processes."[1] Not only did God create us, but He also continues to display His creative genius in our lives through the transforming work of the Holy Spirit. Living no to self provides countless opportunities to embrace the image in which we were created. You might call it our family heritage.

Looking Like Daddy

"She looks like her momma but acts like her daddy." Was that a compliment, or an insult? I wasn't really sure how to receive those words when I was young. My momma is one of the most beautiful women I've ever known (inside and out). My sweet daddy was a looker in his younger years, and he's dapper and rugged in his golden years. As far as acting like my daddy, I chose to receive that as a compliment (and, I will say, I didn't mind being told I looked like my momma), because my earthly father bears a strong likeness to his heavenly Father.

What exactly is our heavenly Father like? And how can we be like Him? We established earlier that the Holy Spirit is part of the Holy Trinity: Father, Son, and Holy Spirit, also referred to as the triune God (*triune* means "three in one"). These three are the Godhead, three in one, and they share the same characteristics. They are our true image consultants. Their attributes should shape our image.

Reflecting our Father's image births a freedom we've never known.

Brother Paul clearly defined how to look like our heavenly Daddy in his letter to the church in Galatia. He had a heart for the region surrounding Galatia, as it was part of his first missionary journey. Many new churches had been established under Paul's leadership, but now a group of Christians called Judaizers were teaching a doctrine contrary to salvation by faith alone.

Paul wrote to correct their wrong teaching and to reestablish what it meant to be a Christ follower. Part of his letter outlined how to live by the Spirit by specifying the characteristics of the Spirit. We needn't look any further than Galatians 5:22–23 to discover the specs of the image we should be transforming into: "But the fruit of the Spirit is love, joy, peace, forbearance, kindness, goodness, faithfulness, gentleness and self-control. Against such things there is no law."

Oh, friend, this is who we were created to be and what God intended for us to look like to the world before sin stepped in and Satan stole our identity. Can you imagine a world filled with believers who lived in this image? Reflecting our Father's image births a freedom we've never known. Since looking like our Daddy is vital to our pursuit of the immeasurably more life, we should park here for a while and make sure we understand what each part of our image means.

Our Image Defined in Nine Words

I want to reaffirm one of the five sustaining truths mentioned earlier: *I was created to be like Him [God].* Repeat that truth out loud. Our enemy is smart and cunning, but he is not all knowing (omniscient). He doesn't know what we are thinking; therefore, if we are only *thinking biblical truths*, we aren't a threat to him. If we want to send him packing, or as my friend Meg says, "Kick him to the curb," we have to speak gospel truth out loud. When Jesus was tempted by Satan in the wilderness, Jesus didn't just *think* truth; He *spoke* truth to the enemy. Notice the exclamation point: "Jesus said to him, 'Away from me, Satan! For it is written: "Worship the Lord your God, and serve him only."' Then the devil left him, and angels came and attended him" (Matt. 4:10–11).

The same authority in Jesus lives in you and me. Isn't that amazing! Girls, Satan only has the power we relinquish to him. When it comes to our image and authority, we have surrendered too much territory to the enemy. Satan has to be put in his place if we plan to have liberty and enjoy life with the God of immeasurably more. Take off your gloves, roll up your sleeves, and put your dukes up! Like the Israelites did when they were rebuilding the wall around Jerusalem as they were released from Babylonian captivity (Neh. 1–8), we have to fight the enemy.

One way to do this is by following God's instructions and pressing toward the goal of saying no to self so that we are transformed and reflect our Father's image. The image we strive to reflect is defined in Scripture in nine words. Let's take a closer look at these, also known as the fruit of the Spirit. Don't worry—there won't be a pop quiz at the end of the chapter!

Satan only has the power we relinquish to him.

Love in the Galatians 5 verse is the Greek word *agapé*. This is a brotherly, benevolent love toward mankind.[2] It's the kind of love that chooses to love even when love isn't deserved. As Bible commentator William Barclay put it, "Agape has to do with the mind: it is not simply an emotion which rises unbidden in our hearts; it is a principle by which we deliberately live."[3]

Joy is the Greek word *chara* and refers to the cause or occasion of joy.[4] For the believer, our joy is generated by the Lord and our relationship with Him. For this reason, it cannot be stolen because of unforeseen circumstances or hardships. It's greater than the thrill of a newborn baby, the graduation or marriage ceremony of a child, or the salvation of a loved one. "Believers are not dependent upon circumstances. Their joy comes not from what they have, but from what they are; not from where they are, but from whose they are; not from what they enjoy, but from that which was suffered for them by their Lord," as preached by Charles Spurgeon, in a sermon from 1881.[5]

Peace is the Greek word *eiréné*, which means "peace and harmony with God" as well as "between individuals."[6] I love the way Barclay defined peace. He wrote that *eiréné* means "not just freedom from trouble but everything that makes for a man's highest good. Here it means that tranquility of heart which derives from the all-pervading consciousness that our times are in the hands of God."[7] Oh, don't we need some of this peace to dissipate all the dysfunction in our world?

Forbearance is represented by the Greek word *makrothumia*. The meaning is as hard to take in as the word is to say. Maybe the phonetic breakdown will help: mak-roth-oo-mee'-ah. From *Helps Word Studies* we find that *forbearance* means "waiting a sufficient time before express-ing anger. This avoids the premature use of force (retribution) that rises out of improper anger (a personal reaction)."[8] I have to confess—this part of my reflection of God's image suffers greatly. Am I alone?

Kindness (or *gentleness*; different translations use this word instead of *kindness*) is the Greek word *chréstotés*, and it refers to "meeting real needs, in God's way, in His timing (fashion)."[9] Kindness is easy to offer to those we love, but difficult to give to those sandpaper-type people in our lives who rub us the wrong way. Kindness is always happy to give to others. It helps us get along with and help others, through Jesus's love in our hearts. God supplies what we need to be kind to all people, even those sandpaper ones.

Goodness is translated from the Greek word *agathosune*. This is goodness "as relating to believers, the goodness that *comes from God* …

and showing itself in spiritual, moral *excellence* (virtue)."[10] Goodness helps us to love the Lord and be obedient to His Word. Through this quality, Christians can live productively and civilly in society.

Faithfulness is the Greek word *pistis*. *Helps Word Studies* defines it as "a gift from God, and never something that can be produced by people."[11] *Martin Luther's Commentary* notes that faithfulness here does not refer to "faith in Christ, but faith in men. Such faith is not suspicious of people but believes the best."[12] Faithfulness believes in the basic good of man and lives life accordingly.

> *Allowing the Spirit to enable us to control the self-seeking and self-serving part of ourselves*
> *is the beginning of our decrease and God's increase.*

Gentleness, also referred to as *meekness*, is the Greek word *praotés*. Gentleness displays "the right blend of force and reserve (gentleness) … avoids unnecessary harshness, yet without compromising or being too slow to use necessary force."[13] Leon Morris in his commentary on Galatians stated, "It is important for the Christian to see that the self-assertiveness that is so much a part of the twentieth-century life should not be valued highly. It is much better that each of us curtails the desire to be pre-eminent and exercises a proper meekness (or gentleness)."[14]

Self-control is the Greek word *enkráteia*. "It is the virtue of one who masters his desires and passions, especially his sensual appetites."[15] David Guzik stated, "The world knows something of self-control, but almost always for a selfish reason. It knows the self-discipline and denial someone will go through for *themselves*, but the *self-control of the Spirit* will also work on behalf of others."[16] Allowing the Spirit to enable us to control the self-seeking and self-serving part of ourselves is the beginning of our decrease and God's increase.

Wow. Nine words really paint a big picture! I'm intimidated by this image we're supposed to attain. How can we be expected to look like our Father if we feel overwhelmed by the image Scripture tells us to reflect? By taking each day and circumstance moment by moment. By choosing to listen to and obey the Spirit's promptings when we'd rather give in to our sinful desires.

> ***It's important to remember—they are called***
> ***fruit of the Spirit, not fruit of the flesh.***

Sometimes I feel accomplished when I don't scream at a driver who pulls out in front of me, smart off to my hubby when he asks "Is there any underwear in the laundry rotation?" or pinch the skin on the back of my seventeen-year-old's arm because of a less-than-respectful reply. I should feel accomplished, and so should you, each time we don't give in to the flesh, because we're reflecting our Father's image. It's not about perfection; it's about progress, and it's about transformation and living out God's active work of Romans 12:1–2. But the weight of the progress can get heavy if we try to make it happen in the flesh all on our own.

It's important to remember—they are called fruit of the Spirit, not fruit of the flesh. We weren't meant to live this life apart from Christ or His Spirit. The progress we make is through His power. The more we say yes to God and no to self, the more we will look like our Father. Living in His image will become second nature. You can choose

- Love—regardless of others' race, religion, ethnicity, gender, socioeconomic status, or any other factor. Rather than standing in judgment or criticism when a person is in need, yield to love, because it's what your Father would do, and you are created in His image.

- Joy—when the bank account is drained, the child leaves home, or the doctor calls and says, "I'm sorry; it's cancer." Rather than despairing over your circumstances, pray and ask God to help you find something joyful on which to affix your gaze, because it's what your Father would do, and you are created in His image.

- Peace—when God chooses not to heal, when a coworker points the finger at you when her mistake is discovered, when your marriage is in trouble … again. Rather than remaining mad or planning retaliation, choose peace, because it's what your Father would do, and you are created in His image.

- Patience—when the peeling of the layers seems to be taking too long, the expected apology never comes, or things don't turn out as planned. Rather than huffing and puffing, display patience, because it's what your Father would do, and you are created in His image.

- Kindness—when others ignore the homeless and outcast. Rather than hoarding what you have, share from your bounty, because it's what your Father would do, and you are created in His image.
- Goodness—when you cancel the movie channels from your cable provider and throw out all your secular fiction books that normalize ungodly behavior. Rather than flirting with the line of purity of mind, body, soul, and spirit, boldly stand on the right side, because it's what your Father would do, and you are created in His image.
- Faithfulness—when your friend fails to call you back or respond quickly enough to a text message. Rather than believing the worst, determine to believe the best, because it's what your Father would do, and you are created in His image.
- Gentleness—as the promotion is given to someone else, another person is living your dream, or you have an opportunity to assert your rightness. Rather than making yourself known, step back quietly to make God known, because it's what your Father would do, and you are created in His image.
- Self-control—the moment you are given the opportunity to satisfy your own needs and wants or to have your own way. Rather than being selfish,

act in a selfless way, because it's what your Father
would do, and you are created in His image.

Seems like a lot of work, doesn't it? Maybe you are asking yourself: *Does all this really matter? Will it really make a difference in my life? Is it worth the investment?*

> **You'll realize that no to self is a great way to live, and**
> **the longing to look like God will become greater.**

Before you know it, people will begin to notice a difference in you. Your disposition will be cheerful, your heart will be happy, and your choices will be God centered rather than self centered. You'll realize that saying no to self is a great way to live, and the longing to look like God will become greater. The yes, no, and maybe disciplines are *more* than worth the investment. I'm living proof, but don't just take my word for it. Let's go back to Damascus and check in with Paul: "Saul spent several days with the disciples in Damascus. At once he began to preach in the synagogues that Jesus is the Son of God. All those who heard him were astonished and asked, 'Isn't he the man who raised havoc in Jerusalem among those who call on this name?'" (Acts 9:19–21).

Paul had the reputation of Christian hater, not Christ lover. Within moments his whole life was changed.

When you decide to say no to self and accept the image God created for you, people will notice the difference. They might even ask superficial questions like "Did you do something different to your hair? Have you lost weight? You seem different; what happened?" The superficial questions will give you the opportunity to share about the supernatural changes a life surrendered to Christ creates. You can tell the secrets of the fruit.

THE SECRET OF EXHIBITING THE FRUIT

My earthly daddy beautifully reflects the image of our heavenly Father. I have watched him exhibit the fruit of the Spirit my whole life. He gave when he had little to spare, served when he was physically disabled, loved when others were unlovable to most, and forgave without reservation when he was hurt. He knew the secret of the fruit; because I didn't know it, he shared the secret with me.

I remember as an elementary-age little girl, after my parents tucked me into bed, they would go back to the family room to hang out, but not before closing the folding hall door. After a short while, I'd quietly sneak down the hall and peek through the slats. (I mentioned earlier that I was nosy.)

Momma would be tidying up (like mommas do), and Daddy would be reading his Bible ... even on days other than Sunday. If I woke up early in the morning, I'd repeat my nighttime ritual and peek through the door; just as the evening before, I'd see my father reading his Bible. When we went on vacation, he would tuck his red New Testament—which usually stayed in his work truck—on the dashboard of our Country Squire wood-paneled station wagon. I was amazed! He read his Bible on vacation. In my mind, Bibles were for church—you took them to church and read them in church. Oh, I'd be remiss if I left my sweet momma out. She knew the secret of the fruit too. When I'd walk into the kitchen in the morning, she'd be having her coffee with Jesus, her green Living Bible lying open on the place mat beside her cup of coffee.

Without ever saying a word, my parents shared with me the secret of the fruit: abiding in Christ. In some of His final words to His disciples, Jesus shared this secret with them. He was preparing the disciples for His death. Jesus wanted to assure them that even though He would be leaving, they could remain close to Him: "I am the vine, you are the branches; he who abides in Me and I in him, he bears much fruit, for apart from Me you can do nothing" (John 15:5 NASB).

According to *Strong's* definitions, the word *abide* is translated from the Greek word *meno* and means "to stay in a given place or state, to continue, dwell, endure, be present, remain, stand, tarry."[17] We are supposed to hang around with Jesus: talk with Him whenever and wherever we go about anything and everything, like we would with our very best friend. Isn't that so cool? And what's even cooler is Jesus hangs around with us.

I have to ask; did you notice the word *fruit* in John 15:5? Yes, it is the same word used in Galatians 5:22, and the definition just might make you stand on your chair and dance a Jesus dance. *Fruit* is the Greek word *karpós* and means "everything done in *true partnership with Christ*, i.e. a believer (a branch) lives in union with Christ (the Vine). By definition, fruit … results from *two* life streams—the Lord living His life through ours—to yield fruit that is eternal."[18] For more fun, check out 1 John 4:17: "This is how love is made complete among us so that we will have confidence on the day of judgment: In this world we are like Jesus." We are meant to be like Jesus.

In the immeasurably more life, Genesis tells us we're made in God's image, Galatians states we are given the fruit of the Spirit, and now 1 John lets us know that we are to be like Jesus—we're to reflect all three persons of the Trinity. Together, they're our image consultant—we're to be transformed into their likeness more and more each day by allowing them to peel off the layers of ugly. So how do we do this?

We are supposed to hang around with Jesus: talk with Him whenever and wherever we go about anything and everything, like we would with our very best friend.

We do what He would do. We learn to be like Him by hanging around with Him. Yes, we have our time when we pray and study His Word, but abiding isn't just for our quiet time. Hanging out means acknowledging Him wherever we are. I love the way *The Message* breaks down Romans 12:1–2:

> So here's what I want you to do, God helping you: Take your everyday, ordinary life—your sleeping, eating, going-to-work, and walking-around life—and place it before God as an offering. Embracing what God does for you is the best thing you can do for him. Don't become so well-adjusted to your culture that you fit into it without even thinking. Instead, fix your attention on God. You'll be changed from the inside out. Readily recognize what he wants from you, and quickly respond to it. Unlike the culture around you, always dragging you down to its level of immaturity, God brings the best out of you, develops well-formed maturity in you.

Oh, friend, Jesus is so fun to hang out with. He loves us so much that He wants to hang out with us too. He wants us to be like our Father, and He will help us mature in our faith. As a result, His Spirit in us will yield the good fruit. The immeasurably more life is unobtainable without abiding in Christ. Jesus knew it. My daddy knew it. I know it. Now you know it. As we abide, revelation is brought to light.

ASK AND IMAGINE

Turn to chapter 10. What will peeling back the layers of the onion reveal in your life? Examine Galatians 5:22–23 carefully: "But the fruit of the Spirit is love, joy, peace, forbearance, kindness, goodness, faithfulness, gentleness and self-control. Against such things there is no law." What fruit shines in your life? What fruit needs to grow?

5

No to Self: Analyzing What Conceals My Image

As I mentioned earlier, a morning quiet time with Jesus and my Bible have been a regular part of my everyday life for quite some time. My time with Jesus is so special that I named a chair after Him. To my family, it is the old, rickety, food-stained blue recliner. But to me it is my "Jesus chair." This chair holds my tears and absorbs my praise. It hears my questions and keeps my secrets. My Jesus chair is where I got to know Him as Lord.

There I have experienced His new mercies each morning when my soul was troubled, became acquainted with His grace when I needed forgiveness, felt loved when I had been treated unkindly, encountered friendship when I was lonely, received peace when I faced a storm, and shared celebrations when I tasted victory. The chair is where I learned all about obedience and overcoming obstacles, and this is where Jesus became my obsession. In the tattered, tear-soaked chair, I learned about my image. Oh, I hope you have a chair like that! Here's the thing: saying yes, conquering obstacles, and reshaping our image is easy to do in our "Jesus chair," but we eventually have to leave our place of comfort and rest with the Lord and face the world—and ourselves.

P IS FOR POSSIBILITY

In chapter 1, at the end of the section headed "Our First and Biggest Yes," I used the word *possibility* in a couple of sentences and later promised to address this word's connection to the immeasurably more life. I am a woman of my word, so let's define the word and then review these statements. *Possibility* refers to something that is capable of being chosen or of being made real.

> The *possibility* of a Spirit-filled life, free from the pulling power of sin, is available to us. But we can't even see that possibility until we accept God's invitation for salvation—our first and biggest yes to God.

This possibility—salvation—*is made real* with the confession of Jesus as Lord and belief that God raised Him from the dead (see Rom. 10:9). We learned in chapter 2: "The moment Paul responded *yes* to God, his old nature—former thoughts and actions—was replaced by a new nature and the *possibility* of new ways of thinking and acting." This *possibility* of new attitudes and actions occurs when we cooperate with the specified work of the Holy Spirit. The immeasurably more life is a real possibility for you and me—if we choose it. It is made real through the power of God—it doesn't have to stay just a dream in your head or a feeling in your heart.

We work against our relationship with God when we refuse to surrender our ways to obey His ways.

When I walked down the church aisle as a little girl, the possibility of my salvation became a reality. On that day, my salvation was secured. While no one can steal our eternal life (see John 10:28–29), someone can stymie us from living the immeasurably more life. This troublemaker is none other than Satan himself. "Be sober-minded; be watchful. Your adversary the devil prowls around like a roaring lion, seeking someone to devour" (1 Pet. 5:8 ESV). Yes, Satan is capable and cunning enough to prohibit our progress. Yet there is another someone; someone I never expected to work against me in my relationship with Christ—me.

We're friends, right? Friends tell each other hard truths in love. This truth is a whammy, so brace yourself. Satan *is* powerful and on a mission to destroy our advancement, but *we* can hinder our spiritual growth too. Let's face it; we are self-willed and stiff-necked. (Take a deep breath.) We work against our relationship with God when we refuse to surrender our ways to obey His ways. Before I began to get serious about my relationship with Christ and started praying the Psalm 139 "Search me" prayer, I blamed every bad happenstance and negative circumstance in my life on Satan. I gave him too much credit, and I never took enough responsibility.

I had made the colossal mistake of thinking that learning God's Word was enough; I never gave any real thought to living the truths

I had learned. My mind was filled with knowledge, but my heart was consumed with me, myself, and I. There are approximately eighteen inches between our head and our heart. The Word hadn't made the trip a foot and a half south yet. I proudly and routinely had my quiet time each morning. I got to know my glorious Savior, but I failed to allow the Spirit to identify areas of my life that weren't in alignment with my new image. Arrogantly, I thought, *This messy life doesn't have anything to do with me. I go to church. I study, underline, and highlight Scripture. I take sermon notes. I sing in the choir—I even perform solos. I tithe. All this mess has to do with everyone else around me. God, fix them.* Boy, was I wrong.

> **The life we want to live, that we were created to live, is found by working in cooperation with the Holy Spirit to become like the One in whose image we were created.**

The distance to the immeasurably more life is paved with God's Word. It took me fifteen years to walk that road, but as I did, Scripture transformed me from being my own enemy. Each time I refused to obey and failed to cooperate with the Spirit's work, the possibility of the immeasurably more life moved a little further out of reach. I wanted the reward without the work.

I'm not suggesting we are saved by works or that the immeasurably more life is a result of them. There is only one way we can receive the gift of salvation or live with the God of immeasurably more—that way is grace. "For it is by grace you have been saved, through faith—and this is not from yourselves, it is the gift of God—not by works, so that no one can boast" (Eph. 2:8–9). Nothing can be added or taken away from the free gift of salvation through faith in Jesus. The life we want to live, that we were created to live, is found by working in cooperation with the Holy Spirit to become like the One in whose image we were created.

When we live in cooperation with the Spirit's work, allowing Him to create new attitudes and actions, the possibility of the immeasurably more life becomes a reality. He reveals what needs to be changed, and He has already provided us with everything we need to make these changes. "For the Spirit God gave us does not make us timid, but gives us power, love and self-discipline" (2 Tim. 1:7).

Can you even believe it! We already have all we need; our job is to surrender to the Holy Spirit's analysis of our life.

It's possible you've already checked out of our conversation with thoughts like: *This life is a possibility, but how? How do I move from here to there? I'm a notorious quitter. I just know I can't do this. I'm too old. I'm too young. I'm too set in my ways. And I'm managing just fine now.* Did I hit the nail on the head? If so, it's because I've been in your shoes and have stood on the brink of this possibility. Take it from this Jesus-adoring, Bible-loving woman: you have what it takes to make living with the God of immeasurably more a reality.

Jesus didn't suffer and die so we could live a "just fine" life.

Maybe you breezed right by the key verse for this portion. I probably would have too, because it is on a mostly blank page. I typically skip those to move on to the reading. Let me share it again. Perhaps you've seen this verse layered over a pretty picture on Facebook or Instagram, heard it on a Christian radio station, or had it quoted to you by your grandma. You may have read it in your Bible, but you've never really believed it applies to your situation. I've included several translations here. Pick one you like. Memorize it. Write it on index cards and place those cards in areas you often see—your car, your bathroom mirror, the kitchen sink, your Jesus chair, your closet, and so forth. Read it out loud. Ask God to help you believe it. He will; He's that faithful. The verse is found in Philippians 4:13.

> I can do all this through him who gives me strength. (NIV)

> For I can do everything through Christ, who gives me strength. (NLT)

> For I can do everything God asks me to with the help of Christ who gives me the strength and power. (TLB)

> I can do all things [which He has called me to do] through Him who strengthens and empowers me [to fulfill His purpose—I am self-sufficient in Christ's sufficiency; I am ready for anything and equal to anything through Him who infuses me with inner strength and confident peace.] (AMP)

Jesus didn't suffer and die so we could live a "just fine" life. He submitted to His Father's will and to a cruel death on the cross so we could live a life abundant, full, and free—immeasurably more than "just fine." That life may only be approximately eighteen inches away. You have the sweet and gentle Holy Spirit as your traveling companion.

The journey is worth the work, even when that work is hard and you encounter the "real you."

ENCOUNTERING THE REAL ME

I wanted a good relationship with God, because I thought that if I had that, everything would turn out okay. A good relationship with God meant my home would become a place my husband wanted to be and our marriage and family would be rock solid. Though a little misguided, there's truth in that optimism. God does cause all things to work for good. "And we know that God causes everything to work together for the good of those who love God and are called according to his purpose for them" (Rom. 8:28 NLT)—but not for the good of those who just want things to be good. My goals were good; my motive wasn't.

The prerequisite to *the good* God causes for us is loving God. I loved God, but not enough to demonstrate that love through complete obedience and submission. Seriously, I didn't even know what all this meant. (These were the early peeling-back-the-onion and give-my-scarf-away days.) I wasn't sure how I would figure it all out; I just knew I was a mess and needed Jesus. Early mornings with my green Living Bible (like the one my momma read), sitting in my Jesus chair, is where I started.

I would wake up at dark-thirty, as we say in the South. When my eyes would pop open, I knew it was the Holy Spirit waking me … and I didn't like it. Yes, I wanted a good relationship with God, but I didn't want it to start so early in the morning. *Why can't I meet with Jesus after the sun comes up?*

After years of rising-with-the-sun moments with Jesus, I now realize I can talk to Him anytime and all the time, but the morning is special. The morning is before the world wakes up and bothers us. It's before the family starts to stir and busyness happens. Scripture tells us about times when Jesus rose early to pray. "Very early in the morning, while it was still dark, Jesus got up, left the house and went off to a solitary place, where he prayed" (Mark 1:35). My friend Lysa says, "We must exchange whispers with God before shouts with the world." The mornings are quiet and just between me and Him. After weeks of my dark-thirty wake-up calls, the Spirit revealed what I didn't expect. Like a Mack truck coming toward me at a crazy-high speed, I saw it—the real me. The me I never wanted to see.

Each morning, as I stomped up the steps to go to my Jesus chair, I would complain. *I just got into deep sleep. Griffin kept me up most of the night. Didn't You see that? This better be good.* Yes, I spoke to the Savior and Creator of the world this way. Now I ask you, would you want to share truths with and answer the prayers of anyone who greeted you with this self-centeredness? I wish I could say I was exaggerating, but that would be a lie. I had asked God to help me, and now I was complaining about His manner of doing so. Mercy, I was a rude, wretched mess; yet God was faithful to meet me each morning. The harsh revelation of the real me became transparent. I didn't have to open my Bible to find a reference for confirmation. The message was clear; however, God resolutely made sure I understood.

No to self invites revelation. We might not like what is revealed, but we can trust God to expose what needs to be exposed, and we can trust His timing in doing so.

My friend Sheri gave me a book, which is funny, because I am not a fan of reading. Reading was one of my poorer subjects in school, and it never got better as an adult. I rarely read for pleasure, so when Sheri gifted me a book with instructions to read only one chapter at a time, I thought, *No problem.* After reading the cover I wondered, *How will I ever read this book if I don't even understand the title?* Panic filled me. Boy, am I thankful I pushed through that panic. That book's message set my life on a course of unparalleled adventure.

God used *I Am Not but I Know I AM: Welcome to the Story of God* by Louie Giglio to rock my world. It is on my recommended must-read list. In fact, I—the woman who doesn't like to read—have read it numerous times. The bottom line is, this story, everything that happens in life, is not about us—it's about God. Your response might be a sweet, patronizing *Duh* because you already know this truth. But as for me? Well, I must have been absent from Sunday school the day they taught this lesson. Louie explained it in short, easy sentences everyone can understand. We are *I am nots* in the story of the great *I AM.* Here, let him tell you:

> God says: I AM the center of everything! I AM running the show! I AM the same every day, forever! I AM the owner of everything! I AM the Lord! I AM the creator and sustainer of life! I AM the Savior! I AM more than enough! I AM inexhaustible and immeasurable! I AM God!!!!!
>
> Just try it under your breath. My name is I am not. I am not the center of everything. I am

not in control. I am not the solution. I am not all-powerful. I am not calling the shots. I am not the owner of anything. I am not the Lord. I am not running anything. I am not the head of anything. I am not in charge of anything. I am not the Maker. I am not the Savior. I am not holding it all together. I am not God.[1]

As we submit, God reveals.

Swallowing the truth of this revelation was like trying to swallow a pill without water. It got stuck and just hung there. *What? This story is really not about me? I'm not in control? I'm not holding things together? I'm not in charge of anything?* I didn't like the sound of that at all! I argued with God about what He was revealing to me. *I'm excellent at being in charge. I have marvelous ideas. I'm a leader; just look at my spiritual gifts inventory.*

To which my sweet, loving, heavenly Daddy replied, "Really? How's all that working out for you?" (my paraphrase).

As we submit, God reveals. Tenderly, the Holy Spirit will expose the areas of our life that do not align with our new image. "And just as we have borne the image of the earthly man, so shall we bear the image of the heavenly man" (1 Cor. 15:49). No to self invites revelation. We might not like what is revealed, but we can trust God to expose what needs to be exposed, and we can trust His timing in doing so. The ultimate goal is to look like our Daddy and to experience the immeasurably more life He designed for us.

A IS FOR ANALYZE

There was no way I could have predicted the outcome of my dark-thirty morning meetings with Jesus. I was ill informed about myself. Life was not about me, my happiness, or my comfort. Poor Jesus. He had to start at the basics with this girl. I can imagine Him looking up at the Father to say, "We've got a long way to go with this one."

I'm thankful that foresight isn't as clear as hindsight, because if I had seen the ride I was about to take, I would have quit before I ever got started. Girlfriend to girlfriend? This journey isn't for the faint of heart, but God knows that you are up for the mission. Others have gone before you and persevered. They serve as examples that saying yes to God and no to self is the only way to fully experience God's richest and most bountiful blessings. God knew that Noah would withstand the test of time to complete the ark, that Moses would get over his stuttering to become a great leader, and that Esther would rise to the occasion to save her people. And He knows you have what it takes to live the plan He created for you.

As I have taken a look back at my journey and studied the steps it took me to accept the new image God had for me, I've realized that the issues that keep us out of alignment with God's plan can be categorized into three concealers: strongholds, self-centeredness, and self-sufficiency. I'm so excited to tell you that the remedy for what conceals our image has already been written. We don't have to search Google or look through our Bible concordance; it is found in a verse we briefly discussed earlier. The correction to our concealers is found in 2 Timothy 1:7: "For the Spirit God gave us does not make us timid, but gives us power, love and self-discipline." Not only do we know what the Spirit does *not* give us, but we know what He *does* give us. Oh, Peter was so right when he wrote, "His divine power has given us everything we need for a godly life through our knowledge of him who called us by his own glory and goodness" (2 Pet. 1:3). Isn't our Daddy awesome! He has already equipped us for success. Praise Him!

Victory is yours! God gives! He gives!

For all the word nerds, this chart is for you. We can't possibly move forward without defining those three *concealers* (thank you, Dictionary.com for helping us with the definitions) and unveiling how God has prepared *correctors* to adjust our misalignment (with thanks to Biblehub.com and *Helps Word Studies*).[2]

Concealers	Correctors
Strongholds: "A well-fortified place; fortress; a defensible place. A place of a spiritual battle."	Power—*dunamis* (Greek): (miraculous) power, might, strength, *power* to achieve by applying the Lord's *inherent abilities*. Power through God's ability.
Self-centeredness: "Moderate concern with one's own interests and well-being; self-love or egotism."	Love—*agapé*: love, goodwill, *love* which centers in moral *preference* on what *God prefers*.
Self-sufficiency: "Having extreme confidence in one's own resources, powers, etc."	Self-discipline—*sóphronismos*: prudent, sensible behavior that "fits" a situation; aptly acting out *God's will* by doing what *He* calls sound reasoning.

Now, for those who are list girls and aren't into word-nerding, here ya go:

- God gives power to defeat strongholds.
- God gives love to neutralize self-centeredness.
- God gives self-discipline to circumvent self-sufficiency.

Are you celebrating yet? Admit it. Go ahead. You were already feeling defeated. The warnings I gave you were intimidating. Now, after reading the chart and the list, you are feeling excited and confident—as you should. Victory is yours! God gives! He gives!

For the remainder of this chapter, we are going to unpack a biblical perspective for each concealer and its corrector. The definitions included in the chart are from an English dictionary, but the Holy Spirit did not inspire that. Therefore, as believers, while it's great to have the knowledge that a dictionary or other resource can provide, it's more prudent to understand what God and His Word have to say about strongholds, self-centeredness, and self-sufficiency.

S IS FOR ... STRONGHOLDS

God gives power to defeat strongholds.

A stronghold is anything that pretends to be true, goes against the truth of God's Word, and strongly influences our actions and attitudes. God's Word tells me in Psalm 139:14 that I am fearfully and wonderfully made. However, because of past failures and not being a very good student, I couldn't believe this truth. *You aren't good enough* was the message that sounded true in my life, and this developed into a defeated mind-set.

Your list of strongholds (aka pretenders) likely looks different from mine; therefore, a comprehensive list isn't possible. Meaningful quiet time with Jesus will help us analyze our individual lives by the light of God's Word to expose anything that is pretending to be true and directing the way we act and think. Paul wrote about strongholds and our actions against them in 2 Corinthians 10:5, "We demolish arguments and every pretension that sets itself up against the knowledge of God, and we take captive every thought to make it obedient to Christ."

The more time we spend with and obey God, the more our confidence in Him will grow. It will take time, but eventually the pretender will be demolished and we will be set free from the stronghold.

> *We can hold the stronghold in the light of God's*
> *Word, but unless we take action to bring it down,*
> *we will continue to be affected chronically.*

The way I see it, this verse is a twofold challenge to the believer. First, we have to know the truth by learning the Word. It's essential to have an understanding of God's position on our stronghold. Don't be alarmed. This doesn't mean we have to memorize the entire Bible. If it did, very few of us would ever abolish any strongholds. Even Christians unfamiliar with Bible study can read a few of Paul's letters and identify the "arguments and pretensions" present in their lives and understand God's thoughts on them. We can search for the pretender using the concordance in the back of our Bible and then look up the verses listed. There are many reputable websites full of free biblical information available for keyword researching. Consider using Biblehub.com, BlueletterBible.org, and GotQuestions.org. Type in the pretender you are dealing with and press enter.

The second part of our twofold challenge is to take action and obey the truth. We can hold the stronghold in the light of God's Word, but unless we take action to bring it down, we will continue to be affected chronically. Let's work through a pretender I've personally struggled with to see how this plays out: *I don't have to forgive someone who has hurt me.*

Here's the nonbiblical view on personal offenses or attacks: *get even when someone hurts you,* and *it's crazy to try to live in peace with anyone who offends you.* A quick search for the word *unforgiveness* in a commentary or on any other websites listed above displays no results; however, a search for "forgive" and "living in peace" shows pages of results. Within just a few moments, I discovered God's position on forgiving others and how He expects me to respond in a crisis of offense.

Here are the truths I found: "Be kind and compassionate to one another, forgiving each other, just as in Christ God forgave you" (Eph. 4:32). "If it is possible, as far as it depends on you, live at peace with everyone" (Rom. 12:18).

So I identified my *concealer*—the stronghold of unforgiveness—and I learned the truth in God's Word: God wants us to forgive as He forgave us and to live at peace with everyone. Now I had to take that truth and turn to God's power to put my *corrector* into practice.

What pretended to be true was exposed and demolished by the light of God's Word before it took root and killed the good fruit in my life.

Many years ago, when my Griffin was about four, he mauled our neighbor's flower bed with his Power Wheels 4x4 truck. I wasn't aware of Griffin's behavior because he had slipped out of the house without my knowledge. Yes, running over the flowers was terrible. Yes, he deserved punishment. No, I didn't deserve to be turned over to the Department of Social Services as an unfit mother. Yes, you read that correctly.

The details of the story are long and intricate and are not pertinent to the stronghold of unforgiveness. My flesh and the world told me to confront my neighbors and tell them off using words not included in the holy canon of Scripture. Unforgiveness pretended to be the truth at the time and directed my actions. With a hateful and hurt attitude, I did exactly what my flesh told me to do—I called all my neighbors one by one to tattle on the tattletales. Thankfully, each call went to voicemail. This afforded me the luxury of time to cry out to God and to give Him my pain. When my neighbors eventually came over to explain, apologize, and ask for forgiveness, my emotions and thoughts had had time to align with God's Word, so I was able to honestly forgive them.

Was this easy? Of course not. Have you dealt with a similar situation? Betrayal is hard to forgive, isn't it? Apart from *dunamis*, the miraculous power, might, and strength imparted to me through the Holy Spirit (according to 2 Timothy 1:7), living in peace with my offenders would have been impossible. Each day when I would turn onto our cul-de-sac, anger would rise up, but my *dunamis* gave me victory. What pretended to be true was exposed and demolished by the light of God's Word before it took root and killed the good fruit in my life.

S IS FOR ... SELF-CENTEREDNESS

God gives love to neutralize self-centeredness.

Oh, wow, we are going deep here, girl. Brace yourself. The Spirit has been working double time and overtime to correct this concealer. First, let's zoom in on a definition. A self-centered person is selfish, full of pride, and is more concerned with how things will or will not affect her than with what happens to anyone else.

Often Scripture comes with a one-two power punch. Paul should have included a warning with this next verse—he wasn't one for mincing words.

> For people will love only themselves and their money. They will be boastful and proud, scoffing at God, disobedient to their parents, and ungrateful. They will consider nothing sacred. They will be unloving and unforgiving; they will slander others and have no self-control. They will be cruel and hate what is good. They will betray their friends, be reckless, be puffed up with pride, and love pleasure rather than God. They will act religious, but they will reject the power that could make them godly. Stay away from people like that! (2 Tim. 3:2–5 NLT)

I feel the need to pause and interject Hebrews 4:12 to help us recall the purpose of God's Word. It is not meant to make us feel good; it's meant to make us act right. "For the word of God is alive and active. Sharper than any double-edged sword, it penetrates even to dividing soul and spirit, joints and marrow; it judges the thoughts and attitudes of the heart." There it is—the process of analyzing our image captured in one verse. It's as if God knew we would one day need it. Imagine that! Analyzing isn't easy—it can be painful! But those who don't analyze never correct and, therefore, are unable to experience the immeasurably more life—a life that is too good to miss.

Even the strongest believer and most fervent Jesus follower struggles with correcting the concealer of self-centeredness.

No one wants to identify with this concealer, but truth be told, we all struggle with self-centeredness on some level. We inherited the sin nature (see Rom. 5:12), and although the penalty of sin (death) has been satisfied, the pull of sin is still alive. We have a choice—to give in to it or deny it. We have the choice to gratify the cravings of our flesh and follow its desires and thoughts (see Eph. 2:3) or to satisfy the Holy Spirit through obedience to God. It's that simple and that difficult all at the same time.

Our flesh and our spirit are always in a battle—and the battle is real. Even the strongest believer and most fervent Jesus follower struggles with correcting the concealer of self-centeredness. Paul confessed his conflict, "For what I want to do I do not do, but what I hate I do.… As it is, it is no longer I myself who do it, but it is sin living in me" (Rom. 7:15, 17). We feel your pain, Paul. We really do.

Let's practice again. I've identified the *concealer* of the image God wants for me—this time, it's self-centeredness: being concerned with my own interests first and over anyone else's. Now I look for God's *truth*: "Do nothing out of selfish ambition or vain conceit. Rather, in humility value others above yourselves, not looking to your own interests but each of you to the interests of the others" (Phil. 2:3–4).

Then I put the *corrector* into practice: love. In chapter 3 I shared the story of the hand-me-downs my friend Stacy had received and given to me for my son, Griffin. If you recall, her kiddos are a little younger than mine. For many years I handed down clothing my children had outgrown to her children. This was a way I could bless my friend who had blessed me in ways other than giving clothes. The system was working well until I started thinking.

> ***Our flesh and our spirit are always in a battle—and the battle is real.***

My momma not only taught me about reading my Bible every day; she also showed me how to shop. I can sniff out a bargain like a hound dog on a hunt. With this gift, I am able to find high-quality apparel for rock-bottom prices. When my babies were little, keeping their clothes in good shape allowed me to consign them to help pay for new wardrobes for another season for my kids. What I didn't consign, I would give to Stacy.

One year I got behind in my closet cleaning and had two seasons of clothes to go through. For an entire Saturday, I separated items into two stacks: a consign pile and a Stacy pile. At the end of the day, I looked at my work and felt quite accomplished. As I organized the groups at the end of the hall, I sensed the Spirit say, *Give them all to Stacy.* Oh, how I wish I could tell you that I zipped my mouth and obeyed, but I didn't.

God, I have to consign this pile so we can buy replacements for Blaire and Griffin. This bag is for Stacy. I'm giving her clothes, but I have to sell these. This conversation serves as an example of how *little* I thought of God's ability to provide for my family and how *much* I thought of my knowledge of our financial situation. He was relentless in His instruction, though, and we repeated this same conversation for well over a week. The mounds stared at me each time I passed them in the hall. I even began to get angry at them and turned away as I walked by. (Seriously, I know. Help me, please.) My heels were dug in deep. I knew if I held out just a bit longer, the Spirit would stop speaking and I would follow through with *my* plan. (I told y'all I was a mess.) You can probably guess what happened. Obedience won. Actually, Stacy's children won, I won, and most of all, God won.

Selfishness obsesses on self while righteousness obsesses on God.

Self-centeredness is a form of idolatry, my friend. We elevate ourselves to be the god of our own life and think we are qualified to make decisions about all things that concern us. I determined I could make a better financial investment with my consigning rather than with my giving. My thoughts were me, mine, and ours. I reasoned, *Aren't we supposed to take care of our children and family?* Yes, but we are also supposed to recognize God as our provider and trust Him to give what we need when we need it. Paul knew this lesson: "In everything I did, I showed you that by this kind of hard work we must help the weak, remembering the words the Lord Jesus himself said: 'It is more blessed to give than to receive'" (Acts 20:35).

As I recall, my children never went without clothing in the season to follow. There wasn't one day either of them walked around naked. Not long after this, I stopped consigning. God clearly directed me to give everything to a charitable Christian organization in my area, unless He specified otherwise. Now I cheerfully give to, pray for, and consider the woman recovering from domestic violence who is wearing one of my blouses to a job interview, or the little boy grinning as he plays in my son's barely-worn-because-he-outgrew-them-too-fast basketball shoes.

Selfishness obsesses on self while righteousness obsesses on God. Our old nature isn't bent to give, serve, and care for others, but our new nature sure is. We just have to lean into the bend. This nurturing, kind, and benevolent brotherly love comes from God. Paul calls it *agapé. Agapé* love looks out for the good of others. It responds in the manner God prefers and is the only way to correct the concealer of self-centeredness.

S IS FOR ... SELF-SUFFICIENCY

God gives self-discipline to circumvent self-sufficiency, which is our final concealer.

When the Spirit's analysis reveals an extreme confidence in our own resources, abilities, and power, then we need to look to God's Word for correction. Remember how I told you that the enemy is out to kill, steal, and destroy? Well, here's a perfect example of his craftiness—he uses the stronghold of self-sufficiency.

Like I said, my mother taught me to be an expert bargain shopper. But what I believe my mom meant for good, the enemy used for evil.

Somewhere along the way, through disappointing times in my life and low self-esteem, I began to see shopping as an escape. It became the way I brought myself happiness. So much so, I entered my marriage in debt and managed to keep us in debt during most of our early years together. The debt I accrued became my secret. I hid credit card bills from my husband, as well as new things that I bought.

Each month, I would scrape enough money together from my household budget to make the minimum payments. I relied on me, myself, and I to make ends meet. Think about how consumed I was with consigning my kids' old clothes. Now it makes more sense, huh?

The lies I repeatedly told Scott kept me from having an honest and open relationship with him. The lies I believed—convincing myself that I could continue with this unwise and out-of-control spending—stopped me from experiencing the real joy that comes with an intimate, dependent relationship with Jesus. My self-sufficiency led me away from the immeasurably more life.

When the Spirit's analysis reveals an extreme confidence in our own resources, abilities, and power, then we need to look to God's Word for correction.

I'm not sure which is worse, self-sufficiency or others-sufficiency. God longs to be our sole provider. He didn't create us with a lone ranger mentality. We were designed to be God-dependent, not self-sufficient. We may be able to make small, short strides in this world, but Jesus said, "I am the vine; you are the branches. If you remain in me and I in you, you will bear much fruit; apart from me you can do nothing" (John 15:5).

Let's do our image analysis one more time. What is the *concealer*? Self-sufficiency—relying on my own resources and power to deal with my problems. What's God's *truth*? "Not that we are sufficient in ourselves to claim anything as coming from us, but our sufficiency is from God" (2 Cor. 3:5 ESV). And finally, consider the *corrector*—self-discipline.

> ### *God provides the wisdom we need to make*
> ### *sensible decisions in every situation.*

My poor husband didn't realize the weight I had put on his shoulders when we exchanged our "I dos." How could he have? I had credit card debt when we married, but I wasn't fully aware of the magnitude of my spending struggles. I didn't start my image analysis, aka praying the "Search me" prayer, until we had been married for almost fifteen years. God revealed my "self-sufficiency." The initial analysis was heart wrenching. The needless anxiety and internal strain Scott must have felt while working hard to provide for our family weighed on me. But to correct this concealer, I confessed to Scott what God had revealed, as well as all my debt, surrendered my cut-up credit cards to him, and asked for his forgiveness for the burden of the displaced responsibility.

With my confession, God slowly began to build my God-fidence. Over time I reclaimed the self-discipline I had surrendered to the enemy. My spending moved from credit card and debit purchases to cash only. Every purchase, even a pack of gum or Dr Pepper, was recorded in a spending log. God replaced my wants of this and that with the joy of financial accountability to Him as well as to my Scott.

The years of morning quiet times, saying yes to God, and declaring no to self had become my self-disciplines. With very little knowledge of

God's Word, and the wonderful and powerful gift of 2 Timothy 1:7, I had opened, applied, and come to appreciate the gift of self-discipline. God provides the wisdom we need to make sensible decisions in every situation. Through prayer and the study of His Word, we can apply His teachings to our life in order to live disciplined lives and be dependent on Him, rather than ourselves.

We can't leave this chapter thinking God only reveals what displeases Him. He is such a sweet and kind Father. Through our obedience, we experience His pleasure. On the days I hit a home run (follow through with the right motive and right attitude), His presence is so real I feel as if I can reach out and hug Him. With my hands raised in praise, I can almost feel His hands joined to mine. The way to living with the God of immeasurably more is paved with experiences like no others. Don't miss the trip!

ASK AND IMAGINE

Turn to chapter 10. A is for Analyze. Spend some time with the concealers.

Strongholds: a well-fortified place; fortress; a defensible place. A place of a spiritual battle.
Self-Centeredness: moderate concern with one's own interests and well-being; self-love or egotism.
Self-Sufficiency: having extreme confidence in one's own resources, powers, etc.

Which concealers are the greatest struggle for you? Why?

6

No to Self: Adjusting to My New Image

Seasons of learning to live the disciplines of yes, no, and maybe can be exhilarating. There's certainly a spiritual thrill associated with walking in tandem with Christ, and simple acts of obedience can result in surprise encounters with facets of Him you've never known.

One Sunday you place a tithe check in the offering at church as you wonder how the power bill will be paid. A few days later you discover God as Jehovah-Jireh—the Lord will Provide (Gen. 22:14)—when you open the mailbox to find a rebate check for the exact amount of your power bill.

Then there are the challenging periods of the journey. Your morning quiet times with Jesus are so precious. His Word is coming alive as your understanding of Scripture deepens. Yeses are exciting, and noes are becoming easier, but things aren't changing. As in a new marriage, new job, or moving to a new town, there is a period of adjustment, shifting away from the things of this world and moving toward the things of God's Word.

Paul warns us not to conform or adjust ourselves to this world or its ways. We learned Romans 12:2 earlier, but let's have a refresher: "Do not conform to the pattern of this world." A look at the word *adjust* in Dictionary.com will amaze you: it means "to change (something) so that it fits, corresponds, or conforms."[1] Paul continues in Romans 12:2, "But be transformed by the renewing of your mind. Then you will be able to test and approve what God's will is—his good, pleasing and perfect will." Wow! When we refuse to conform to the world and when we adjust to God's ways, we please Him. I can hardly take it in!

> *Being caught between the charms of our culture*
> *and the wooing of the Spirit can be toilsome.*

Adjustments can be exhilarating and exhausting at the same time. As we conform to God's image, and the things of the flesh lose their grip on us, we often have to make practical changes in our life that require time and energy. Maybe you find yourself not so popular at work because you no longer watch the offensive show everyone talks about. You no longer participate in the community gossip that's commonly heard at your hair salon, so you look for a new stylist in order not to be tempted to fall back into old ways. Being caught between the charms of our culture and the wooing of the Spirit can be toilsome. Rest assured, all you are experiencing is for your good. God *is* at work, even when it seems everything is changing.

But let's be honest: too much change at once can be too much for a girl, especially when it involves lipstick, lotion, and food.

CHA-CHA-CHA-CHANGES

My signature shade of lipstick was Chocolate Mousse. Momma had taught me how to line my lips and apply lipstick flawlessly; Mary Kay had provided the perfect color. One morning, as I rolled up the tube to paint my lips, I noticed that I needed to reorder. However, I wasn't prepared for the disturbing news I received from my representative: my favorite shade had been … *discontinued.*

Shocking, right? The story gets worse.

My daddy built custom homes for a living. His hands were soft as velvet and callous free, even though his profession demanded physical labor. Besides the Bible on the dash of his truck, my dad kept a bottle of lotion in the front seat. He was determined to have soft hands (perhaps for my mom). I picked up this same determination from my father and carried it into adulthood, when I found and fell in love with Vaseline Intensive Care Firming and Nourishing Moisturizing Lotion (let's face it, when a girl approaches forty, certain areas on her body aren't as toned as they once were). One day, when I pressed the pump and nothing came out, I headed to the store to replenish my stock. Much to my dismay, the store was out of my favorite cream. After stopping at another store and seeing that they, too, did not have it on their shelves, I asked the clerk when a new shipment would arrive. That's when I heard that unpleasant word yet again—*discontinued.*

Are you feeling my pain? Hang on, it gets even worse.

When your children are little, eating out without them is a luxury. Scott and I didn't pamper ourselves very often, but when we did, we indulged at Raucci's. Raucci's didn't hand out a place mat and crayons.

White cloths covered the tables, candles lit the room, and peaceful piano music filled the air. Raucci's was our place, until it—oh yes—*closed*.

While I was chasing God, the Spirit was changing me.

The lipstick, the lotion, and the restaurant were things of the world. Small, simple, nonspiritual things, but I wanted to hold on to them. They felt safe, secure, and certain when bigger things were falling away, as I adjusted to the order God had prepared for me. Fearful of the uncertainty, I cried out to Him: *Why? Why do things have to change? I know I'm being silly, but help me understand.* As only a faithful and loving Father could do, God reassured me with certainty from His Word:

- *I am certain*: "Jesus Christ is the same yesterday and today and forever" (Heb. 13:8).
- *I won't ever change*: "I the LORD do not change" (Mal. 3:6).
- *I will always be with you*: "Be strong and courageous. Do not be afraid or terrified because of them, for the LORD your God goes with you; he will never leave you nor forsake you" (Deut. 31:6).

This biblical reassurance offered great comfort as I transformed. While I was chasing God, the Spirit was changing me. My temper no longer seemed to be winning; there were no new holes in the walls (like the one I had created with my foot in a moment of rage). Wisdom made itself obvious to me when I needed to make a decision or respond to a situation: *Yes, you are right, but keep your mouth closed.* Knowing that the Lord was by my side gave me courage to keep changing. Trusting God through obedience had become an exciting way to live.

> *It's impossible to hold hands with the world*
> *and the hand of God at the same time.*

The closer I drew to the Lord, the further I receded from the world. But I'll be honest, there was a part of me that wanted both—to be accepted by others and by God. To read the Word and experience its power, yet *not* to be challenged by it in my daily living. To enjoy the blessings of following God without giving up the pleasures of world. But we can't have the world *and* the ways of God.

It's impossible to hold hands with the world and the hand of God at the same time. To live with the God of immeasurably more, we have to release our grip on the things of this world and take hold of our identity as co-heirs with Christ: "The Spirit himself testifies with our spirit that we are God's children. Now if we are children, then we are heirs—heirs of God and co-heirs with Christ, if indeed we share in his sufferings in order that we may also share in his glory" (Rom. 8:16–17). And since we are co-heirs with Christ, it's time we act like the heirs that we are: "Those who live according to the flesh have their minds set on what the flesh desires; but those who live in accordance with the Spirit have their minds set on what the Spirit desires" (v. 5).

If you're uncertain, fearful, and don't like change, then highlight the verses of reassurance from a few paragraphs above. We can be certain that all the Spirit's adjustments are making us like our Father. "And we all, with unveiled face, beholding the glory of the Lord, are being transformed into the same image from one degree of glory to another.

For this comes from the Lord who is the Spirit" (2 Cor. 3:18 ESV). Don't miss the amazing words "being transformed." This phrase in the original Greek is *metamorphoó* (met-am-or-fo'-o) and, according to *Helps Word Studies*, combines two meanings: "*change after* being *with*" and "changing *form* in keeping with inner reality."[2] The word *being* is a progressive present-tense verb, meaning it is happening now. We *are becoming* like our Father. As we spend time with Him, His Word is teaching us; His Spirit is directing us.

THE WORK OF THE WORD

Even though things were changing and were difficult at times, my growing relationship with Christ thrilled me. My Memory Bank of Faith overflowed with God's faithfulness. Instead of stomping up the steps for my quiet time in the morning, I leapt out of bed to meet with Jesus. Our time together helped me slay my old image, as we critically analyzed things in my life that were keeping me from embracing my new image. Slowly but surely, God was becoming my magnificent obsession.

Here's the thing about obsessions—you can never get enough of them. This being true, how do we get more of God? We get more of God when we give God more of us. I can't explain how giving means getting, but in the economy of God, it works. Oh, does it work! Our sacrifices—the giving up of our wants, whims, and wishes to obediently follow God's ways—cause us to depend on and draw close to Him. And God? Well, He draws close to us too. It's a beautiful thing. "Draw near to God, and he will draw near to you" (James 4:8 ESV). This exchange is worth all the adjustments we make and all the training we endure.

We get more of God when we give God more of us.

NBA Hall of Famer Michael Jordan, arguably one of the greatest basketball players to date, didn't just show up on the floor of the United Center and say to the head coach of the Chicago Bulls, "Hey, I wanna play ball." Before Jordan could play in the big leagues and lead the Chicago Bulls to six NBA titles, he had to spend years training. In fact, before he landed a spot on his high school basketball team, he had to put in loads of work. Jordan didn't even make the Emsley A. Laney High School varsity team at first. As reported by the *Newsweek Special Edition*, "'Whenever I was working out and got tired and figured I ought to stop, I'd close my eyes and see that list in the locker room without my name on it,' Jordan would explain. 'That usually got me going again.'"[3]

Mia Hamm is widely known as one of the greatest female soccer players in the history of the game. She led her alma mater, the University of North Carolina at Chapel Hill, to four consecutive NCAA women's championships. Hamm won two Olympic gold medals in soccer and was a two-time FIFA World Player of the Year, despite being born with a club foot.[4]

How did these two famous athletes make it to the top of their sports? Training—lots and lots of training.

Paul applies the same discipline to our relationship with God through Christ. And he gives another key to the immeasurably more life in 1 Timothy 4:8: training for godliness. "Physical training is good, but training for godliness is much better, promising benefits in this life and in the life to come" (NLT).

Maybe you relate with me and don't enjoy physical activity. Or you may love to work out and even run marathons for fun. I know exercise releases something called endorphins that are said to make you feel good. Apparently, they make you want to exercise more—again, something that I haven't learned to appreciate. However, the benefits of spiritual exercise that Paul mentions should spur us all—athletes or not—on to "training for godliness."

Godliness sounds a little daunting and like an unattainable goal; let's study the word so we aren't intimidated. *Godliness*, or *eusebeia* (yoo-seb'-i-ah), means "someone's inner response to the things of God which shows itself in godly piety (reverence)."[5] The end goal of godliness sounds awesome, something we'd all stand in line to receive: "benefits in this life and in the life to come" (1 Tim. 4:8 NLT). But the training? Well, that's the part that can trip us up.

For an athlete, when the going gets tough, the tough keep going. They do all the things necessary to accomplish the goal of being the best. Some believers have a different mind-set when it comes to training (in godliness): when the going gets tough, just give up. But we can't give up! There's too much at stake, and God left us a training manual with inspiring verses to help us as we strive to reach our goal.

> *When our Memory Bank of Faith is full, and we experience the tenderness of the feel-good words, we can accept the tough words and joyfully submit to godliness training.*

The Scriptures are the inspired work of God, and they're good for us in numerous ways. Let's explore four of those ways: "All Scripture is inspired by God and profitable for *teaching*, for *reproof*, for *correction*, for *training* in righteousness; so that the man of God may be adequate, equipped for every good work" (2 Tim. 3:16–17 NASB). The key words in these verses are charted below for easy understanding.[6]

Teaching	Reproof
(*didaskalía*/did-as-kal-ee'-ah) giving instruction	(*elegchos*/el'-eng-khos) reproachment or conviction
Correction	Training
(*epanorthósis*/ep-an-or'-tho-sis) restoration to the proper condition	(*paideia*/pahee-di'-ah) instructing someone to reach maturity

I'll go ahead and put it out there: these are tough words to invite into our vocabulary and our relationship with God. As I said at the beginning of the book, we often find it easier to embrace feel-good Bible words like *love, grace, mercy,* and *forgiveness* rather than words that challenge us. That's why it's important to top off our Memory Bank account with remembrances of God's goodness and the knowledge that His work is a good thing. When our Memory Bank of Faith is full, and we experience the tenderness of the feel-good words, we can accept the tough words and joyfully submit to godliness training.

TRAINING IN ACTION

God works in real time. It's important to have your prayers said, Bible read, and sins confessed so you don't miss one minute of His perfecting work, even if it's not something you think needs to be accomplished. I can relate to that last part especially. One day, I checked my email with the goal of clearing out my inbox. I had no thought of God using an email to clean out and correct my heart. I simply wanted to open my email, not an invitation for correction.

But we never know who our active and always-working God will choose to accomplish His work. Many times, without our knowledge or consent (not that He needs it), He invites skilled individuals into our godliness training. They suit up and join His team to help shape us to walk confidently in our new identity. God used Linda in this way in my life a few years ago. And let me tell you, I never saw her coming!

It's important to have your prayers said, Bible read, and sins confessed so you don't miss one minute of His perfecting work.

Blindsided. That's how I felt when I met my "sharpener." King Solomon speaks of the benefits of sharpeners in Proverbs 27:17, "As iron sharpens iron, so one person sharpens another." Apparently, it was time for refining, and God sent the refinements directly to my inbox. Her emails were short and blunt. You know, the kind of matter-of-fact tone your best friend has earned the right to use because she's been in your life for twenty-plus years.

But this woman was not a friend; in fact, I barely knew her. She had attended an event where I had spoken, and she had decided to join my online Read Thru the Word class. What she didn't understand was that her membership in the class didn't come with an all-access pass to send me *correcting* and *training* messages. Her communications played like staccato notes on the keyboard. One after another, she critiqued my video teachings:

- "The lighting in that room isn't favorable."
- "You should probably get a mic. It's hard to hear when you fluctuate your voice."
- "Consider taking Maxie's dog collar off. She jingles when she's in the room."
- "The room with the bricks is the best for sound and light."
- "Don't sit in front of that mirror. You look like you have horns on your head."

You get the picture. Now, you may be wondering, *Why didn't you block her? Did you tell her off in a Christian, bless-your-heart kind of way?* The answer is complicated.

A few years prior to my encounter with this bulldozer, I had begun praying Proverbs 15:31, "If you listen to constructive criticism, you will be at home among the wise" (NLT). I'll go ahead and confess, I really only wanted God to grant me the second half of the verse, "to be at home among the wise." My life had been surrounded and encouraged by many wise people. Their influence stirred a desire in me to be wise, but I did not want to be criticized in order to become wise. (For the record, we don't get to pick and choose which half of a verse we want to live out. It's an all-or-nothing deal.)

You see, my prayer for wisdom included criticism, and that meant I shouldn't block or delete Linda's emails. And as much as I wanted to give her a good ol' southern "bless your heart and butt out," God reminded me of Proverbs 15:31. In a way only God could arrange, the wisdom I had desired was wrapped up in the criticism I detested.

*Being corrected and rebuked isn't fun, but it is necessary
if we want to live in the likeness of our Father.*

A wise person evaluates each criticism they receive for truthfulness, and then they respond. Based on my assessment of Linda's statement, she was right. Sharp in tone, but on point. Therefore, it was easy to conclude that her emails weren't meant to trash me, but to train me. Little did I know that God had given her the assignment of helping me hone my video-teaching skills. Under her advisement, my videos improved in quality, becoming sharper and more professional. What started out as a *Who in the world does this lady think she is?* relationship has turned into a friendship and ministry partnership. Linda's attention to detail makes her the perfect speaking assistant for me. And to think—I almost deleted her constructive criticisms!

God may use many sources to bring His useful Word to our mind. He can even use ungodly people and situations to train us. When the lady in the post office is rude and not afraid to let you know she thinks you cut in line, you realize the usefulness of Psalm 141:3, "Set a guard over my mouth, LORD; keep watch over the door of my lips."

God provides us with instructions for godliness. He also gives us the teaching material (His Word), as well as the Teacher (His Spirit), to help us make the proper adjustments to confidently live out our new image. The way we respond is our decision.

Being corrected and rebuked isn't fun, but it is necessary if we want to live in the likeness of our Father. The training words in 2 Timothy sound difficult and laborious. My first reaction to them isn't to jump up and down and say, "Pick me!" But when I pause to consider that training produces godliness, which causes me to better reflect my heavenly

Father, then I'm filled with joy. So much so that I do want to shout, "Pick me!" And of course, living the powerful reality of 2 Timothy 3:16–17 is made easier when I know I have the Helper.

THE WORK OF THE SPIRIT

I'm so excited about this leg of our journey. As we strive to become more like Christ and to learn from God's Word, we will need an exceptional teacher. One who shows mercy, but whose standards remain steadfast; who demonstrates love, while hating our sin; and who offers forgiveness, without excusing our behavior.

God provided the perfect teacher in the person of the Holy Spirit. You met Him on your Damascus road experience. He stirred your heart when Jesus was seeking you. He's part of the Trinity (Father, Son, and Holy Spirit).

> *Jesus died for so much more than our salvation.*

He is already part of your life, made possible through the death, burial, and resurrection of Jesus. "Nevertheless, I tell you the truth: it is to your advantage that I go away, for if I do not go away, the Helper will not come to you. But if I go, I will send him to you" (John 16:7 ESV). He has been with us since our salvation experience, but sadly our recognition of our relationship with Him often begins and ends at that point, because we fail to realize His desire to be part of our daily life.

Jesus died for so much more than our salvation. Remember John 10:10: "The thief comes only to steal and kill and destroy; I have come that they may have life, and have it to the full"? Jesus came so we could have more—*immeasurably more*. And the Teacher, the Holy Spirit, helps us live in the *more*.

Here are some things we need to know about this amazing person:

- He's also called our advocate and advisor. His job is to teach us about right and wrong. "And when he comes, he will convict the world of its sin, and of God's righteousness, and of the coming judgment" (John 16:8 NLT).
- His power in us is not limited. "For the one whom God has sent speaks the words of God, for God gives the Spirit without limit" (John 3:34).
- He will guide us in truth and tell us what we need to know. "But when he, the Spirit of truth, comes, he will guide you into all the truth. He will not speak on his own; he will speak only what he hears, and he will tell you what is yet to come" (John 16:13).
- He is a beautiful gift from God. Peter said, "Repent and be baptized, every one of you, in the name of Jesus Christ for the forgiveness of your sins. And you will receive the gift of the Holy Spirit" (Acts 2:38).
- He speaks to the Father on our behalf concerning our prayers. "In the same way the Spirit also helps our weakness; for we do not know how to pray as we should, but the Spirit Himself intercedes for us with groanings too deep for words" (Rom. 8:26 NASB).

The Holy Spirit is the perfect person to help us make the adjustments necessary to live fully in our new image. I mean, if the Spirit is good enough for Paul, He's good enough for me, right? Remember, when we were last with Paul, he had accepted his new identity with great confidence; however, people were still skeptical of the new and improved Paul. He had gone to the synagogues in Damascus and was preaching the good news that Jesus was the Son of God.

We need to press rewind just a bit to discover the source of Paul's preaching authority: "Then Ananias went to the house and entered it. Placing his hands on Saul, he said, 'Brother Saul, the Lord—Jesus, who appeared to you on the road as you were coming here—has sent me so that you may see again and be filled with the Holy Spirit'" (Acts 9:17).

All of Paul's knowledge of the Word did him little good without the indwelling of the Holy Spirit. This is true for every person; we need the Holy Spirit. And here's the good news: the same Spirit that filled Paul fills you and me. The same Spirit who equipped Paul to do all things equips you and me. The same Spirit who taught him to imitate Christ teaches us.

Paul knew he wasn't alone in the race he was running. God is so incredibly generous not to leave us alone, floundering around, trying to live a life that pleases Him. Can you believe it? God is in us through the person of the Holy Spirit. "For God is working in you, giving you the desire and the power to do what pleases him" (Phil. 2:13 NLT). Mind blown!

The Holy Spirit is the perfect person to help us make the adjustments necessary to live fully in our new image.

THE SPA—THE SPIRIT'S PERFECTING ADJUSTMENTS

Are you a "why" and a "how" girl? Some women can go with the flow and simply trust God. Oh, how I admire those individuals! God is sweet to put up with inquisitive daughters like me. When I inquire of God, I'm not questioning His ability or sovereignty. My questions are more about the procedure and order of how things will shake out. He has my heart and my complete trust, but the nosy part of me loves to have details.

One of my favorite things about our Teacher is His willingness to satisfy (though He doesn't have to) my desire to understand how He works. He connects His actions with everyday life experiences. I remember asking, *Lord, how does Your Spirit work? Help me understand.* The analogy He provided was too good not to share: the Spirit is like a massage therapist—the best one you could ever find at the best spa in the world. He can work as intensely in our spirit as He desires, but He is gracious to invite us into the process and work on us at a pace we can handle. How deep are we willing to let Him go?

One day I'd love to go to a spa for a full day of beauty treatment—I think. To be honest, though, I'm not sure exactly what a full day of beauty treatments involves. However, I have had massages, and I do like them. Massage therapy has proven to be invaluable to people's overall health and well-being. Have you ever had a massage? Usually it involves sitting or lying down while someone rubs, kneads, pushes, and pulls your muscles (or lack of muscles in my case!) in ways to promote circulation and get rid of all those tense knots that form when your teenager won't text you back on a Friday night and he's out past curfew. There are numerous types of massages and relaxation techniques. We are going to have some fun by showing the likeness between the Swedish massage, deep-tissue massage, and pressure-point massage and the working of the Spirit.

We can be confident in the effectiveness of our massage therapy, because we can trust the One touching us. He is an expert and desires that we be spiritually healthy in mind, body, and soul. At a spa, individuals determine the intensity of the work by selecting which type of massage they'd prefer. Our Therapist affords the same option to us. It's very important to read the descriptions carefully before making your selection.

THE MASSAGE: SWEDISH

A Swedish massage can be gentle and relaxing. The therapist uses long, smooth strokes, kneading, and circular movements on the *superficial* layers of muscle. The Swedish massage is the most *common* type of massage therapy.

The Likeness

When we first notice the Spirit's work in our lives, we may only pay attention to what's happening at the surface level—how we feel about some of the everyday sins we engage in. These might be things we don't even see as all that harmful at first. Let's take a closer look at the words *superficial* and *common*. Dictionary.com defines *superficial* as near or related to the surface or shallow, and *common* as ordinary.[7] While a Swedish massage is beneficial in loosening places of tension and restoring some blood flow, the work is shallow. It only touches the surface of the tension, never getting close to the most troubled areas.

The Application

My mouth has always gotten me into trouble—*always*. Every report card in elementary school was marked C in the area of conduct. Each teacher, in her own sweet words, let my parents know I talked entirely too much. The problem persisted into adulthood, when I knew bigger words, had an opinion on everything, and lacked a filter. I would argue with a lamppost until the sun came up. Gossip ran rampant from my tongue. If I heard it, I repeated it—in love, in concern, in a prayer request. Sickening, I know.

The Spirit convicted me of this *common* problem. He reminded me of His teaching: "Don't spread gossip … treat others fairly and don't say cruel things" (Ps. 15:3 CEV). Like the Swedish massage delivers direct relief, confession of my gossip and unfiltered murmurings, and then God's forgiveness, applied respite to my soul. Yet even though I had acknowledged my sin, I didn't change my behavior. The next time the opportunity came to share my unfiltered, opinionated thoughts, I gladly obliged.

The Spirit is always at work but will not bully or overpower us.

THE MASSAGE: DEEP TISSUE

A deep-tissue massage is targeted, well, deeper. The fingers of the therapist *focus* down into all those places that are *chronic* trouble spots in our muscles and apply *more intense* pressure. With the correct amount of pressure and work in the troubled and tight places, *circulation* improves. With improved circulation (internal changes), mobility is restored and stress is reduced.

The Likeness

The Spirit is always at work but will not bully or overpower us. We have the freedom to accept or reject His work. In order to experience the immeasurably more life Jesus died to give, we must yield to the intense work He wants to do. Accepting and analyzing our new image isn't enough. At this stage in our journey, we have to pay attention to the Spirit's *focus* on our *chronic* sin and character flaws. With the correct amount of *intensity*, the *circulation* of His Spirit within us will improve and our likeness to our Father will become more apparent.

The Application

Repeated confession of the same sin became tiring to me and made me ever thankful that God is longsuffering. The frustration of continuing in this pattern of sin and the simple "I'm so sorry, Lord" prayer failed to bring peace to my guilty heart. Finally, in an effort to overcome my *chronic* issue, I sought the Lord for something *deeper*, a tool that would rebuke me in the act of sin. Faithfully, He answered. Like a Dramamine patch on the arm of someone at sea, I covered my heart with Ephesians 4:29, "Do not let any unwholesome talk come out of your mouths, but only what is helpful for building others up according to their needs, that it may benefit those who listen."

The Spirit's work intensified. He pressed deeper to arrive at the core of the problem. My mouth was the superficial issue; the pressure of the Spirit's conviction revealed the source of sin: my heart. *It goes deeper than this, Wendy. What goes in your heart and mind comes out of your mouth. For your mouth speaks from the overflow of your heart* (see Luke 6:45). *Change your television channel and radio station. Find something godly to read. Stop following the links that lead you to places you shouldn't go. When you put better stuff in, better things will come out.*

Yeah, I know, ouch.

Obeying these instructions challenged my very foundation. They turned everything upside down. New music? New shows? Inexplicably, in giving God authority to mess with my mess, joy began to fill my heart. Internal attention showed external changes. Songs of encouragement played in my head; black-and-white television shows of yesteryear entertained me. Less screen time equaled more time with my family. My words were softer and kinder. Responses to stressful situations were handled with a pause and reflection. The intensity of the deep, focused work of the Spirit is well worth our commitment to our new image.

The Spirit's work internally will be evident externally.

THE MASSAGE: PRESSURE POINT

The pressure-point massage, besides just being relaxing, is based on the idea that parts of the foot connect to other parts of the body. As the therapist *manipulates* the foot, pressure is placed on *specific* areas to stimulate blood flow and better functioning of certain organs. A foot massage can also be a way to help people when other types of massage might not be possible because of areas of the body being wounded or *diseased* or otherwise inaccessible.

The Likeness

At times the Holy Spirit will draw our attention to *specific* areas of our lives that require *manipulation* in order to heal our *diseased* hearts. My mouth was the *specific* area that required *manipulation* in order to heal the pride and selfishness of my heart.

The Application

Years of not filtering what went into my heart and mind resulted in unfiltered conversation, opinions, and diatribes. By no means am I a poster girl for the "Completed and Successful Work of Ephesians 4:29" patch, but I've undergone remarkable improvement. The Holy Spirit bore witness to the progress and increased the intensity: He applied the pressure of accountability to my mouth.

Recently, I repeated something slanderous I'd seen on Facebook about a person in ministry. Even with a commitment to the Spirit's work, we sometimes still fail, yet His tender mercy continues to draw us to His perfecting adjustments. How great is His grace!

Several months passed, and it came to my attention that what I had seen wasn't true. Did you know everything on the Internet is not true? (Insert wink.) The pressure of accountability gripped my heart. Immediately, I sought God's forgiveness. As before, He graciously forgave my sin, and I felt His pardon and understood these specific corrective instructions: *This information did not build up or benefit anyone. Set things right with the person to whom you repeated this information.*

> **The intensity of the deep, focused work of the Spirit is
> well worth our commitment to our new image.**

God's grace was sufficient in helping me obey His instructions, without pause, cause, or clause. When I saw Susan, I confessed my sin; with compassion and grace, she forgave me. That moment had to be one of the most humbling moments of my life. But it pleased my Father, and for a brief moment I reflected Him to another person. Wow!

AFTER THE SPA

The funny thing about massages is even though they can be painful, the more you go, the more you want to go. You discover the tension in your shoulders and knots in your back aren't released with only one visit. In order to make a lasting difference in your health, continual visits may be necessary. Spiritually speaking, the same principle applies. Lasting effects of the Spirit's Perfecting Adjustments occur when we continually submit and cooperate with the work He longs to do in our life. Daily appointments with Jesus, an active prayer life, and time in God's Word support the Spirit's work. Before you know it, the new nature supersedes the old nature, and pleasing your heavenly Father becomes more important than pleasing yourself.

The Spirit's work *internally* will be evident *externally*. With His teaching, reproof, correction, and training, spiritual flexibility will no longer be tolerated, and chronic propensity to sin weakens. At this place in our journey, common isn't acceptable and superficial isn't enough. Spiritual adjustments are welcomed rather than avoided. We will crave spiritual things and focus our attention on heavenly investments rather than earthly returns. Our yeses have cultivated a trust relationship with God. By saying no to self, we've invited and assumed our new image. Now, we're ready to consider how *maybe* welcomes freedom.

ASK AND IMAGINE

Turn to chapter 10. In 2 Timothy 3:16–17 (NASB) we read: "All Scripture is inspired by God and profitable for teaching, for reproof, for correction, for training in righteousness; so that the man of God may be adequate, equipped for every good work." How do you respond to the Spirit's work in your life?

Teaching: giving instruction
Reproof: reproachment or conviction
Correction: restoration to the proper condition
Training: instructing someone to reach maturity

Section Three

Maybe Welcomes Freedom

Now the Lord is the Spirit, and where the
Spirit of the Lord is, there is freedom.
2 Corinthians 3:17

7

Maybe Celebrates Freedom For

Growing up I often heard three words *yes*, *no*, and *maybe*. I never had to doubt what my parents meant when they said yes or no. But *maybe*? Well, *maybe* was a mystery. No one wants to hear maybe as a response. The word leaves us in limbo, uncertain of how to proceed. *Maybe* makes us feel held between two worlds: one of opportunity, the other of disappointment.

My parents knew the secret packed in this powerful, short word, yet they never told me. However, in my years of walking out yes and no, God kindly unlocked the mystery of maybe for me. And because we are friends, I'll share the secret with you. To the casual observer, *maybe* feels indeterminate, but the word can do something with certainty—invite freedom and flexibility.

Our friend Paul certainly embraced his liberty in Christ. After his Damascus road experience, a brief convalescence period at the house of Judas, and healing from Ananias's hands (see Acts 9:10–19), Paul hit the gospel road with abandon. We learned earlier how

Paul immediately started preaching (v. 20), and even when his life was threatened, he continued to preach (vv. 23, 29). His freedom led him to complete three missionary journeys and radically turned the faith of the Gentiles and the Jews topsy-turvy. God used Paul's upbringing and his frightful past to change the course of history for the church.

Paul's example of living freely in Christ to serve others should be the goal of every believer. He knew his freedom wasn't for himself, but to spread the gospel of Jesus Christ: "For you have been called to live in freedom, my brothers and sisters. But don't use your freedom to satisfy your sinful nature. Instead, use your freedom to serve one another in love" (Gal. 5:13 NLT).

To the casual observer, **maybe** *feels indeterminate, but the word can do something with certainty—invite freedom and flexibility.*

Thus far, we have redirected any previous notions associated with yes and no. In the final leg of our journey, we are going to take a fresh look at the concept of the word *maybe*. *Maybe* will fill our mind, body, soul, and spirit with peace, and perhaps even cause the corners of our lips to turn up so others around us will think we are up to something. With this word tucked in our vocabulary, decisions will be made with godly confidence and authority. *Maybe* won't just be lip service we give to someone who asks us to do something. *Maybe* will be a welcomed part of our life with the God of immeasurably more—the God who shows us what *may be* if we follow Him. Inhale *maybe* and exhale freedom—freedom in Christ.

FREEDOM *FROM* OR FREEDOM *FOR?*

What comes to mind when you hear the word *freedom?* Go ahead and take a few minutes to think about it. Perhaps patriotic images of flags and the pomp and circumstance of hometown parades celebrating a nation's birth. Maybe the privilege to pursue personal dreams or express your ideas and opinions without restriction or interference. Possibly financial independence. Freedom may mean life without confinement—unbound by bars, a diseased body, or physical abuse. And it's probable that for some now reading this, freedom is just beyond the horizon, or even not at all likely. What if you considered the idea of freedom as freedom *for* something rather than freedom *from* something?

Freedom *for* something is applicable to everyone, no matter their circumstances. Even those who are experiencing financial limitations, physical restrictions, or any other encumbrances can live in freedom *for.* Freedom *for* says what's ahead of me is an opportunity rather than an obligation. There's hope, possibility, and optimism in freedom *for.*

When I started this pursuit to know God more than fifteen years ago, I never imagined I would love God, Jesus, and the Holy Spirit as best friends, savor every morsel of the Word as my daily ration of food for the soul, or experience an inexplicable peace when making decisions, much less have the confident freedom to accomplish whatever God calls me to do. "Immeasurably more than all we can ask or imagine" were pie-in-the-sky words in a Bible verse that I could only find using my table of contents or concordance. All I wanted was for my family to be fixed—you know, to be "normal"—and for the haunting of the thirteen words to fade.

*What if you considered the idea of freedom as freedom
for something rather than freedom from something?*

Honestly, this is how I saw things playing out for my life: my dedication to prayer and the Word would make God *sooo* proud of me. While we enjoyed each other (me getting everything I asked for because I was praying and reading the Bible), He would change my husband's heart to want to be at home more. Any fallout from Scott's unhappiness, our financial challenges, my children's behavior and sleep issues, and other life pressures would naturally be corrected.

It never occurred to me that God's goal was not to make me happy but to make me holy. "But as the One Who called you is holy, you yourselves also be holy in all your conduct and manner of living" (1 Pet. 1:15 AMPC). If I had known at the beginning of the pursuit what the journey would require of me, I probably would have said, "Never mind. I'll just live with the ways things are." And if I had said "Never mind," I would have missed the greatest love story of my life. I would never have experienced and understood what our freedom as believers is *for*.

All of our yeses and noes come to fruition in our *maybe*. As we say yes to God, He becomes our magnificent obsession. The trust relationship with Him is rock solid. Adjustments in our image have been and will continue to be made, because we're saying no to self and becoming like our Father. The teaching, reproof, correcting, and training are all for our freedom. We don't have to be concerned whether saying *maybe* will result in something good. With God, the outcome is always good, even when it doesn't look like it: "And we know that God causes all things to work together for good to those who love God, to those who are called according to His purpose" (Rom. 8:28 NASB).

As GotQuestions.org puts it, "In Romans 8, Paul contrasts a life lived in selfishness pursuits (the flesh) and one lived in league with, or in accordance with, God (the Spirit). He impresses upon readers that our sovereign God is all-knowing, all-wise, and all-powerful. Those who love God can trust His goodness, His power, and His will to work out all things for our good. We journey together with Him."[1] All our work—the yeses, noes, training, and adjustments—has taught us how to be triumphant over the pursuits of the flesh and to live in accordance with God, in His purpose. We have full Memory Banks. Therefore, we can boldly celebrate the promise of Romans 8:28. Maybe celebrates freedom *for*.

> ***All of our yeses and noes come to fruition in our* maybe.**

FREEDOM FOR RADICAL LIVING

Recently I celebrated fifty years of life. When facing a milestone birthday, I tend to do a lot of reflecting on my younger years. Take hairstyles, for example. Oh, the '80s and the *big* hair. In most of my pictures, I look like I am peering through thick shrubbery. Eye shadow had to be frosted, lips painted red, crocheted warmers covered my legs from the ankle to the knee, jeans looked painted on, and cheeks were streaked with pink rouge.

For some, our stereo blasted heavy metal music that our parents hated and said was laced with satanic messages. Many of us spent Friday nights at the home football game and the after-game dance. Social media wasn't on the horizon (and all God's girls collectively say a hushed "hallelujah"). Many movies were acceptable for audiences of all ages. Curse words were something that you spelled or whispered; you did not speak them as part of everyday conversation, especially if you were a lady. They were not commonplace in movies and network television.

Sports teams didn't have practice on Wednesdays so the athletes could attend their local churches. Churches began to open Family Life Centers to attract the community to the campus so people could hear the gospel and see that Christians are just people who love others and Jesus. Families went to church together on Sundays. Youth groups had camp, cookouts, and lock-ins. Church leaders never wavered in their belief of the inerrancy of Scripture. God said it; we believed it—period. Sanctity of life mattered from conception to the grave. A wedding ring meant until death do you part, and it signaled to the opposite sex that "I'm not available."

Fast-forward a few decades. Fashion has been on the decline, not because of what is worn, but because of what is not worn. This book is rated E for everyone, so I won't provide details. You can reread the previous paragraphs, apply the extreme opposite, and you will define our culture today. What happened? Radicalness happened.

Truthfully, radical ideas and trends have always been around. The definition hasn't changed; society and what it deems acceptable has changed. Let's consider the word *radical*: favoring drastic political, economic, or social reforms.[2] Since the existing political, economic, and social views reflect pleasing man and self, and dishonoring the Bible, Christians must declare themselves *radical*. We must favor extreme changes. Our primary goal needs to be for Christ to be "magnified" in our bodies "whether by life or by death" (Phil. 1:20 NKJV). This is freedom *for* radical living.

Radical living risks reputation and rejection for the cause of Christ.

Paul had a great response to freedom for radical living. Recall in Acts 9 where we read about his sight being restored and how he'd started preaching in Damascus. Keep in mind, he had been originally planning on going to the town to capture Christians, and now *he* was a Christ follower—talk about radical! Even though Paul had a new image, he had the same old reputation. People questioned his motives and threatened his life.

> Isn't he the man who raised havoc in Jerusalem among those who call on this name? (Acts 9:21)

> After many days had gone by, there was a conspiracy among the Jews to kill him, but Saul learned of their plan. Day and night they kept close watch on the city gates in order to kill him. But his followers took him by night and lowered him in a basket through an opening in the wall.
> When he came to Jerusalem, he tried to join the disciples, but they were all afraid of him, not believing that he really was a disciple. (vv. 23–26)

> So Saul stayed with them and moved about freely in Jerusalem, speaking boldly in the name of the Lord. He talked and debated with the Hellenistic Jews, but they tried to kill him. When the believers learned of

this, they took him down to Caesarea and sent him
off to Tarsus. (vv. 28–30)

I wonder if Paul considered a maybe. "*Maybe* I should stay around,
even though the disciples don't trust me … even though the message
of Christ is being debated … even though my life is being threatened."
Paul embraced freedom *for* radical living. He favored extreme changes
in the existing views and systems of his day. Radical living risks reputation and rejection for the cause of Christ.

Paul took the message of the gospel on the road, literally. He
completed three intense missionary journeys fulfilling God's call on
his life: "Therefore I want you to know that God's salvation has been
sent to the Gentiles, and they will listen!" (Acts 28:28). Paul suffered so
much—physical abuse, prison time, shipwrecks, harassment, attempts
on his life, blindness, and much more—all as he attempted to live out
God's command to spread the gospel. Because of this murderer turned
evangelist, the early church was strengthened, and the gospel of Jesus
was advanced, despite the existing views against it.

The freedom that *maybe* welcomes cares more about obeying God
and living for Him than fearing the negative repercussions from others. Unlike Paul, not all are called to risk life and limb to advance the
gospel. Some are called to proclaim the good news quietly within their
homes by leading Bible studies. Others may witness to their neighbors
by bringing meals when they're sick. And some folks live radically in
the public eye.

Tim Tebow, Florida Sports Hall of Fame member, former National
Football League quarterback, and Heisman Trophy winner, started a
kneeling craze called Tebowing, an action that now has its own website.

To *Tebow* is "to get down on a knee and start praying, even if everyone else around you is doing something completely different."[3] When radical faith met football, people didn't like it. Tebow received what could be referred to as a "public flogging" for radically standing against existing views of his public demonstrations of faith, even sparking another movement called Tebowing hating. Tebow's response? "It's just my way of humbling myself and thanking my Lord and Savior for all the blessings in my life. The fact that prayer is being talked about is pretty cool."[4]

Television and film actress Candace Cameron Bure is no stranger to radically going against current cultural trends. She boldly accepted a seat around the conversation counter on the controversial talk show *The View.* Among several hosts of varying backgrounds and beliefs, Bure exemplified Romans 1:16: "For I am not ashamed of the gospel, because it is the power of God that brings salvation to everyone who believes: first to the Jew, then to the Gentile." Sitting elbow to elbow, she went toe to toe with liberal public figures, including her cohosts, and she never watered down her faith.

> *The freedom that* **maybe** *welcomes cares more about obeying God and living for Him than fearing the negative repercussions from others.*

Even though our platforms are different from those of Paul, Tebow, and Bure, we are all called to share the gospel, and we're expected to live a life worthy of our calling: "As a prisoner for the Lord, then, I urge you to live a life worthy of the calling you have received" (Eph. 4:1). And what is our calling? Jesus defines it clearly.

Jesus commissioned believers as He prepared to ascend to heaven: "Then Jesus came to them and said, 'All authority in heaven and on earth has been given to me. Therefore go and make disciples of all nations, baptizing them in the name of the Father and of the Son and of the Holy Spirit, and teaching them to obey everything I have commanded you. And surely I am with you always, to the very end of the age" (Matt. 28:18–20).

Paul lived freedom *for* radical living more effectively than any other figure in the New Testament, except Jesus, of course. He lived his life, not for the approval of man, but so that men and women would see Christ exalted in his deeds and words. This caused him to be imprisoned for years, to be beaten, and to be falsely accused. Yes, our radical living might invite rejection by men; however, we have all been appointed and trusted to share the gospel. Maybe you are thinking, *I'm not skilled. I don't know enough. What if I can't answer the questions I'm asked? Rejection hurts.* If Christ has saved you, you are qualified and approved by God to share the gospel. "As we have been approved by God to be entrusted with the glad tidings (the Gospel), so we speak not to please men but to please God, Who tests our hearts" (1 Thess. 2:4 AMPC). And when God examines, or "tests," our hearts, He hopefully will discover love.

FREEDOM *FOR* LAVISH LOVING

Love. Songs are sung, poems are penned, and movies are made, all for the sake of love. Lives are lost, new life is created, and quotes are stated, all in the name of love. Love comes in every language. The daughter in a home with a thatched roof and dirt floor in Mozambique caring for her aging mother loves just as deeply as the daughter feeding her cancer-stricken mother ice chips in the ICU of a top-rated medical center in America. Love lifts. Love leads. Love loses. Love wins. Love takes. Love gives. Perhaps the most famous words ever written concerning love were penned by our friend Paul.

You may be familiar with 1 Corinthians 13:1–7. Perhaps a minister read it at a wedding you attended. Indulge me, please. Read this passage slowly and aloud. There's just something so sweet about reading God's Word out loud. Oh, how I wish we could read it together!

> If I speak with the tongues of men and of angels, but do not have love, I have become a noisy gong or a clanging cymbal. If I have the gift of prophecy, and know all mysteries and all knowledge; and if I have all faith, so as to remove mountains, but do not have love, I am nothing. And if I give all my possessions to feed the poor, and if I surrender my body to be burned, but do not have love, it profits me nothing.
>
> Love is patient, love is kind and is not jealous; love does not brag and is not arrogant, does not act unbecomingly; it does not seek its own, is not provoked, does not take into account a wrong suffered, does not rejoice in unrighteousness, but rejoices with the truth; bears all things, believes all things, hopes all things, endures all things. (1 Cor. 13:1–7 NASB)

Love lifts. Love leads. Love loses. Love wins. Love takes. Love gives.

Let's get the backstory on this amazing poem of love. First Corinthians is one of two letters Paul wrote to the church he had started in Corinth. He had received reports of sexual immorality, pride, and misuse of spiritual gifts, and his letters were an attempt to get the people back on track. In 1 Corinthians 12, we read how Paul refreshed the people's memory of the benefit of spiritual gifts to the church body. He reminded them that these gifts are from God and should be used in an orderly manner. Then—drumroll, please—he breaks out into these beautiful words of chapter 13: "If I have all the spiritual gifts God has to offer, but I don't have love, then I have nothing" (my paraphrase).

Love conquers all—well, it would, if we would just love. Paul is speaking of *agapé* (ag-ah'-pay) love in this letter. This love is the active love of God for His Son and His people, and the active love His people are to have for God, one another, and even enemies.[5] It's Christ's love in us; it's not a love we can manufacture with human effort. *Agapé* love is birthed from a heart that loves God. All the yeses, noes, and training we've had up to this point are worth this love, because we now have the freedom *for* loving lavishly those who need love, as well as those who are hard to love.

Demonstrating *agapé* to our friends, family, and even people we don't know tends to come naturally to many folks. Taking meals to those who are hungry. Praying with and for those in our community with special needs. Helping to care for the yard or home of neighbors during a time of crisis. Offering financial support in a season of loss. These are examples of active love for people we generally care for. However, *agapé* love also includes loving *even our enemies*. Paul defines *love* in 1 Corinthians 13, and he gives details about how to treat our enemies in Romans 12:19–21:

Do not take revenge, my dear friends, but leave room
for God's wrath, for it is written: "It is mine to avenge;
I will repay," says the Lord. On the contrary:

"If your enemy is hungry, feed him;
if he is thirsty, give him something to drink.
In doing this, you will heap burning coals on his head."
Do not be overcome by evil, but overcome evil with good.

Living with the God of immeasurably more means
no longer seeking personal pleasures or agendas,
but living for Him who died and rose again.

Enemy is the Greek word *echthros* (ech-thros') and means one who
is hostile, hating, and opposing another.[6] According to Paul we are to
love anyone who demonstrates hostility, hate, or opposition toward
us. So, when the Spirit leads, we are supposed to bake a cake, make a
meal, offer comfort in loss, provide help in need, and show love and
not animosity for anyone who opposes us. Let's all agree that love like
this is beyond what we are capable of giving, right?

But we are living the immeasurably more life and are free *for* just
this kind of love. So how do we pull this off? "For the love of Christ
controls us, having concluded this, that one died for all, therefore all
died; and He died for all, so that they who live might no longer live
for themselves, but for Him who died and rose again on their behalf"
(2 Cor. 5:14–15 NASB).

Living with the God of immeasurably more means no longer seeking personal pleasures or agendas, but living for Him who died and rose

again. Freedom *for* lavish love does not come from us, but from Christ in us, who works in us to do His will. It's both perplexing and exhilarating at the same time! *Agapé* extends beyond good deeds and acts of kindness to another form of sacrifice: forgiveness. Paul speaks about forgiving those who have offended us in 2 Corinthians 2:10–11: "Anyone you forgive, I also forgive. And what I have forgiven—if there was anything to forgive—I have forgiven in the sight of Christ for your sake, in order that Satan might not outwit us. For we are not unaware of his schemes."

Oh, this is so much easier to say than to do—privately and publicly. Now just imagine being publicly offended in front of millions—yes, millions—of people. Like many others did, my family enjoyed the reality show *American Idol.* Season five introduced an amazing singer to the stage, Mandisa Hundley. She was new to the *Idol* stage, but not to my heart. Her worship at the Living Proof live events with Beth Moore and Travis Cottrell had been blessing me for years. I was utterly thrilled to see her, a singer of contemporary Christian music, become a fan favorite and advance week after week on the television show. Though she wasn't voted as the top American Idol that season, I believe she was the *real* winner. Here's why.

During Mandisa's audition, judge Simon Cowell made a rude and tasteless remark concerning her weight, "Do we have a bigger stage this year?" When asked about the comment, Mandisa shared her heart with reporter Raquel Dunn from CBN: "It was my worst fear come true … because it's been the biggest struggle of my life and because it's something I feel so vulnerable about. For him to have said that and for it to air on national television—I was devastated."[7]

But Mandisa continued competing with grace and style. One particular episode, she walked across the large room to hear whether she would be part of the top twenty. Sitting face to face with her offender, in front of millions of people, Mandisa was given the opportunity to live freedom *for*.

> Simon, a lot people want me to say a lot of things to you. But this is what I want to say … Yes, you hurt me, and I cried, and it was painful. It really was, but I want you to know that I've forgiven you, and that you don't need someone to apologize in order to forgive somebody. And I figure that if Jesus could die so that all of my wrongs could be forgiven, I can certainly extend that same grace to you. I just wanted you to know that.

That's what freedom *for* lavish love can do. It gives us the ability to accomplish the impossible, all in Jesus's name and through His power. He gets the glory and we get the good. The welcome of *maybe* is freedom our soul has longed for. We can love the lovable, as well as those we think aren't lovable, show kindness to those we feel don't deserve it, and forgive our offenders. Lavish loving opens our hearts and hands to experience freedom *for* generous giving.

FREEDOM FOR GENEROUS GIVING

My daddy was a modest man who made a modest income. He never had ambitions to be rich and famous, have a financial portfolio, or have a fancy office with "CEO" on the office door. No, he only wanted a few dollars in his worn-out wallet, to be able to drive his truck until the wheels fell off, and to work hard every day until he physically could not. He benevolently gave to anyone in need: family, hitchhikers (back in the day), the hungry, the poor, widows and children, church folks, and unchurched folks. This daddy of mine lived the immeasurably more life right in front of me, and until this very moment, I never put it all together (*praise You, Jesus*).

Yes to God, no to self, and yep, my parents enjoyed the freedom of maybe for a long time. In all the years I lived under his roof, I never knew my father to miss a tithe. My parents trusted God with their finances and generously gave to others.

Then Hurricane Hugo slammed the Carolinas on September 22, 1989. The devastation was horrific in our city. Debris lined the streets for weeks, and neighbors rallied to help one another. My daddy was a general contractor, so when the city restored power and cleared the roads, the phone starting ringing. One particular job he accepted changed our lives forever.

My father was up on the roof when he fell and broke his leg. It was the worst break the orthopedic surgeon had seen. His first recommendation was to amputate from the knee down. After prayer and lots of consultation, we opted for my dad to undergo a surgery to repair his shattered ankle and badly broken leg. The surgery was followed by months of therapy and no guarantee of real success. The doctor forecasted that my dad would not be able to return to work for at least one year, if ever.

Our family was without words—and an income. But we didn't worry; God had always blessed the work of this hardworking carpenter. Daddy was faithful to God, and we knew God would be faithful to us. We didn't know how, but we knew Who.

Worker's comp paid 30 percent of my daddy's salary, but that was hardly enough to live on (my mom's arthritis kept her out of the workforce). To help with expenses, I moved back home from college rather than living on campus. We did all we could to minimize our spending. One evening while my mom was writing out the bills (these were the pay-by-check and snail-mail days), I noticed a check to our church. I questioned her, "Mom, why are you tithing? God knows Daddy isn't working. Do you really think He still expects you to tithe?" Her reply: "You can't outgive the Lord."

It wasn't long until I learned the reality of her words. While my parents faithfully continued to tithe on a reduced income, ten couples in our church committed to cover the 70 percent income loss that worker's comp did not pay for an entire year. This is the greatest testimony of generous giving I've ever witnessed. My parents gave exponentially, and it was given back exponentially.

When approached about giving, most people think about money. Some may think that if you don't have money, then you have nothing to give. However, generous giving means more than opening our wallets. While some have the financial means to give extraordinarily, others have talents and time they can offer.

Generous giving means more than opening our wallets.

Jesus is our best example of giving, don't you think? He never collected a paycheck and didn't own a home or anything of value. Despite His meager means, He gave what He had: love, compassion, time, and of course, healing. Jesus spent time having dinner at His friends' homes (Luke 10:38–42), as well as religious leaders who sought to discredit Him (7:36). He invested time even with those who opposed Him.

Freedom *for* generous giving isn't only about money. Being a good steward of all that you have and having a willingness to make investments in the kingdom of God help provide you with opportunities to give generously. Consider babysitting for a young couple in your church who are financially unable to pay for a sitter. Invest in a relationship with a college student who is far from home and needs a little TLC. Offer to help in your community's food bank on a weekly basis. Open your home to host a small group. Take a church bulletin to a shut-in and spend some time talking with her about the Sunday service.

An investment of time and talents is just as valuable as money. Additionally, it's not just about what you give; it's about the heart behind the giving. In Paul's second letter to the church in Corinth, he talked about a group of individuals with a huge heart for giving. For the second time, He was asking them to give money for Christians in Jerusalem who were in need. In an effort to spur them on, he boasted about the acts of gracious giving of the Macedonian churches (Philippi, Thessalonica, and Berea)—who, by the way, were very poor.

> And now, brothers and sisters, we want you to know about the grace that God has given the Macedonian churches. In the midst of a very severe trial, their overflowing joy and their extreme poverty welled up in rich generosity. For I testify that they gave as much as they were able, and even beyond their ability. Entirely on their own, they urgently pleaded with us for the privilege of sharing in this service to the Lord's people. (2 Cor. 8:1–4)

An investment of time and talents is just as valuable as money.

Let's pay close attention to several key words and phrases in this passage. *In the midst of a very severe trial. Extreme poverty.* These phrases describe the living conditions of those who called it a privilege to share. *Welled up in rich generosity.* It would have been easy for the churches to write a reply to Paul that sounded like this: *Dear Paul, we are struggling here too. There's really no way we are going to be able to give anything right now. In fact, if you can do some fundraising over this way, we'd sure appreciate it.* Instead, Paul bragged about the Macedonians' giving. Even in lack, they gave as if they had plenty. These churches exercised freedom *for* generous giving.

The freedom welcomed by our *maybe* motivates us to put down our phones and computers to develop real relationships that are unconcerned about likes, emojis, and memes. Relationships nurtured in real time rather than FaceTime. Freedom *for* inspires us to double the recipe and share it with a neighbor or to buy two winter coats at the sale—one to keep and one to give away. Freedom *for* helps us celebrate that we're not consumed with freedom *from* something. It allows us to joyfully embrace maybe, knowing that in God's economy, maybe is something good.

ASK AND IMAGINE

Turn to chapter 10. What most excites you about freedom *for*: radical living, lavish loving, or generous giving? Why? In what ways (if any) are you already demonstrating these in your life?

8

Maybe Considers before Committing

My then six-year-old daughter sounded the alarm as she ran through the house, "Momma, a hummingbird is trapped in the garage. A hummingbird is trapped in the garage!" *Great. Just what I need. I'm already late, trying to get out the door for church, and now I have to deal with a stuck bird.* The anxious voice in my head immediately switched to the calm "Everything's gonna be all right" mom voice, as I assured my daughter we'd rescue the bird. As we walked out to assess the situation, I found myself wondering, *How do you get a bird out of a building?*

The poor bird frantically flew from one closed window to the other closed window, trying to escape its accidental captivity. *Aha! I'll open the windows.* But my tiny feathered friend must have felt threatened rather than relieved by my assistance, because she perched herself on the motor of the garage door opener and ignored the open windows. Operation Hummingbird Fly Home attempt 1: fail. My mind quickly regrouped.

Move the van. Yes. The door opening is larger than the window opening. Even after I removed her biggest obstacle, my little birdy still couldn't figure out how to find the freedom made available to her. She continued to flit and flitter, more anxiously than before. Why couldn't she work it out? Maybe her mind was wrought with worry. Perhaps physical exhaustion had clouded her reasoning and kept her from seeing the way of escape in front of her. Rather than breaking free, she remained panting on top of the motor box. Operation Hummingbird Fly Home attempt 2: fail.

My heart raced as I tried to formulate another plan. I cried out, *Lord, I have to get this bird out of here. I have to get to church. My class will be waiting.* In the pause of the prayer, the Lord gave me another idea. It was the best yet. God was a genius!

I grabbed the broom and held the straw bristles near her tired body in the hope that she'd step on them and allow me to carry her to freedom. Sadly, the poor thing interpreted my offer of help as a threat. She erratically flew faster from window to window, but higher this time, hitting her head on the ceiling, as if to say, "Don't hurt me! Don't hurt me!" By this point, my heart was breaking, my kids were in tears, and I felt certain the bird was crying too. In a strange way, I began to feel a kindred spirit with this little hummer. She was worn out … and so was I. My exhaustion didn't stem just from being Wendy the Bird Rescuer, but from all the commitments piled on my plate. In a similar way to our feathered captive, I felt trapped and in turmoil.

I told the kids to go inside so the bird could calm down, and with tears pouring from my eyes, I sat down. *I get it, Lord. I'm caught up in the captivity of activity. Help me slow down … and help me set this bird and myself free.*

In one final attempt, I slowly lifted the broom under my feathered friend's fragile feet. Her worn-out body fell on the straw bristles.

Motionless, she sat on the broom as I carefully carried her to freedom. *Fly away, friend. So wonderful to meet you today. Thanks for the lesson.* Operation Hummingbird Fly Home attempt 3: success!

> **As we learn to live and enjoy the liberty found in freedom for, it's easy to get caught in the trap of freedom to do.**

I would have never scheduled a life-altering encounter with God and a hummingbird forty-five minutes before the time to leave for church. But clearly, I needed a visualization of my current lifestyle. It was time to pause and *consider* all my assignments: my freedom *for* had become freedom *to do.* My proverbial hat rack was full: wife to Scott, mother to Blaire and Griffin, operating manager of the Pope household, friend, daughter, women's ministry director, Bible study leader, Proverbs 31 Ministries speaker, author, and part-time employee. (Whew! I'm fatigued just typing that list.)

As we learn to live and enjoy the liberty found in freedom *for*, it's easy to get caught in the trap of freedom *to do.* Our love and excitement for the Lord generates a desire to spend all our energy on Him. In our zest to fully experience every aspect of our new image and the immeasurably more life, we become entangled with commitments and strangle the freedom. In being obsessed with freedom *for*, we can spread ourselves so thin that we become busy, but not effective. If we aren't careful to consider reasonable assignments, we may become resentful of all assignments. And when resentment sets in, we fall short of our primary assignment: to glorify God. "Whatever you do, do it all for the glory of God" (1 Cor. 10:31). Our overload slowly affects our productivity, and then our relationships.

If we aren't careful to consider reasonable assignments,
we may become resentful of all assignments.

The lesson I learned from my little hummer friend had a profound effect on me. In the weeks following our encounter, I began to pray and seek the Lord about my captivity of activity. The revelation was eye opening. I had never intended to be so busy serving others that I had little left for those I loved the most. My family received leftovers: leftover creativity, leftover energy, and leftover joy. Yet they were also on the front line to receive my temper, anxiety, and short-fused responses. I finally made the connection between my overzealous desire to embrace my freedom with Scott's thirteen words: "You don't make our house a place I want to come home to." Even today, the words still sting.

No wonder the man didn't want to come home. After working hard, he faced my snippy and snappy comebacks, anxiety rather than peace, and anger instead of joy. You want to know the saddest part of this story? I was having quiet times with Jesus every day. The transformation taking place inside my heart had not translated to those I loved the most because I had fallen prey to another one of Satan's tactics: busyness. Perhaps the late Adrian Rogers, former pastor of Bellevue Baptist Church in Memphis, Tennessee, said it best, "If Satan can't make you bad, he'll make you busy."[1]

Consideration is the bridge between frenzy and freedom for.

In our journey to live the immeasurably more life, we've learned the importance of being real with God about sin, submitting to the training and teaching of the Holy Spirit, and staying in the Word. Our focus is on holiness and resembling the image of our heavenly Father.

We have to be aware that pursuing righteousness and walking in God's truths makes Satan furious. When we're not sinning, the devil knows it, so he will get to us through busyness.

The immeasurably more life isn't rushed; it's relaxed—relaxed in a confident faith that God will direct us to the right ministry assignments and guard us from the wrong ones. This is something I had never considered, which was a costly mistake. Rather than seeing the best of God's work in me, my family saw a "hummingbird mom" stuck in and frenzied from service, with little left to give to her greatest ministry assignment, her family. My humming-bird friend taught me a great lesson while perched on the motor box. She taught me to pause and *consider*. Call me silly, but I think she considered her options and accepted the best one. Consideration is the bridge between frenzy and freedom *for*.

CROSSING THE BRIDGE

What good is freedom *for* if we can't enjoy it? Who decided ministry and life are races meant to be rushed rather than experiences designed to be relished? How different would the flow of our life be if we chose to consider? To consider is to think carefully, contemplate, and reflect on something in order to make a decision.[2]

Careful contemplation isn't something that comes naturally for many people, nor is it a concept widely embraced. Hurry. Hurry. Hurry. Rush. Rush. Rush. Our streets and highways are full of individuals needing to be somewhere *yesterday*. We no longer enjoy the simple pleasure of a leisurely meal. Texting has replaced calling, and emailing is preferred to writing a letter. If we're living at such a fast pace, then why should our decision process be any different?

Before compromising the calmness of freedom for, we must
consider our people, our schedule, and our giftedness.

Consider says, "Wait a minute, there's too much at stake for me to make an uninformed, rash decision." Before compromising the calmness of freedom *for*, we must consider our people, our schedule, and our giftedness, and cover every decision in prayer.

CONSIDERATION IS COVERED IN PRAYER

"I'll pray about it" seems to be the standard Christian response when someone asks us to serve. This is the best response we can give—but only if we actually follow through on it. Prayer can't be our flippant response when we know we don't want to or aren't able to serve. If we say that we will pray, we should pray. With so many opportunities to serve the kingdom of God, how does one choose when, where, and whether to serve?

It's imperative we understand that we have a part to play,
but we aren't responsible for fulfilling every role.

The number of people who need to know the love of Jesus is vast. Our churches need small group leaders, ushers, parking lot assistants, welcome desk volunteers, and the list goes on and on. Church ministry is in-reach focused, but there are a countless number who need ministry outside the church. Outreach ministry takes care of the homeless, girls facing crisis pregnancies, those in the hospital, or people who may need a ride to church.

After feeding the five thousand, Jesus sent out seventy-two men in pairs to serve and to be His witness. In His instructions Jesus said, "The harvest is great, but the workers are few. So pray to the Lord who is in charge of the harvest; ask him to send more workers into his fields" (Luke 10:2 NLT). There will always be a great need. It's imperative we understand that we have a part to play, but we aren't responsible for fulfilling every role.

I love that Jesus's instructions included prayer. Prayer is the first step in considering. Jesus said since the need is great, we need a lot of workers. In prayer, we give God the magnitude of the need and ask Him to help us determine our role. Remember, God will direct us to the right ministry assignments and guard us from the wrong ones; all we have to do is ask. Prayer is how we ask, and listening to God is how we know. It's in the pause of praying and listening to His Word that we can discern His direction.

CONSIDER YOUR PEOPLE

I deliberately chose the word *people* rather than *family* in the above subhead. Family looks different in every community and in every culture, so we will define your *people* as anyone or anything that depends on you for care. Your people may be a combination of children and a husband. It's possible your people include aging parents, a disabled sibling, or a shut-in you've adopted. And yes, let's face it, when we say our "people," we mean our pets too. In our consideration, we look at all our dependents and ask, "How will this affect them?" "What preparations need to be made before accepting the assignment?"

You've been waiting, praying, and saving for years. Finally, the planning meeting for the church's mission trip to Nicaragua is scheduled. With excitement, you continue to pray and pray, but one of your parents begins to have health issues. After many visits to several doctors, the diagnosis of dementia is given. The no-to-self training of the Holy Spirit kicks in. You decline going to Latin America and trust God for another opportunity to serve on the foreign mission field. Saying no to self has become second nature and brings immense joy. In saying maybe, we consider how an impeding decision will affect those around us, and consistently evaluate how current decisions might be affecting them as well. Consideration means willingly making adjustments as necessary or declining the opportunity altogether.

My encounter with my tiny feathered friend made me aware of adjustments I needed to make. It's hard to admit this, but I never considered my people before I started serving as the women's ministry director. My lack of consideration had caused me to compromise the calm in my home. My busyness had tipped the scales of balance. It was obvious that my husband knew it. Even if he couldn't identify the root of the problem, his thirteen words pinpointed it. My children weren't old enough to verbalize their feelings, but as I remember their anxious attitudes and disappointed faces every time I said, "We gotta go," the memory speaks volumes. My service to our church made them resentful of church.

Considering our people demonstrates love and reminds them of their value. Love is also revealed in how we schedule our time.

As I invested time into prayer and consideration, it brought me to the obvious conclusion: someone else could lead the women's ministry, but no one else could be a wife to Scott or a momma to my kids. In order to bring calm to the chaos my overextended service had caused, I announced to my women's ministry team that I would be stepping down when my term concluded. The peace that filled my soul assured me I had made the right decision. No matter what season of life you are in or what ministry opportunity you have in front of you, taking time to consider your people is the only way to maintain balance and peace.

Paul appeared to live most of his life as a single man, yet he had many people to consider. He started churches all over Asia Minor and Europe, and he didn't stop caring about the people in these congregations. He made return visits to them in his missionary trips, and he stayed in touch with them through letters and other missionaries. Paul faithfully remained supportive of Timothy and Titus, two men whom he mentored. Even when he was in prison, he wrote letters to encourage his people. Considering our people demonstrates love and reminds them of their value. Love is also revealed in how we schedule our time.

CONSIDER YOUR COMMITMENTS

Perhaps the most well-known passage and prescription for schedule planning is found in the book of Ecclesiastes. We have to travel to the Old Testament to discover this truth written by King Solomon, but it is worth the trip:

> There is a time for everything,
>> and a season for every activity under the heavens:
>> a time to be born and a time to die,

a time to plant and a time to uproot,

a time to kill and a time to heal,

a time to tear down and a time to build,

a time to weep and a time to laugh,

a time to mourn and a time to dance,

a time to scatter stones and a time to gather them,

a time to embrace and a time to refrain from embracing,

a time to search and a time to give up,

a time to keep and a time to throw away,

a time to tear and a time to mend,

a time to be silent and a time to speak,

a time to love and a time to hate,

a time for war and a time for peace. (Eccl. 3:1–8)

We don't have to read between the lines or decipher a code to discover the truth the wise king wants us to know. In fact, verse 1 is his message in a nutshell: "There is a time for everything." In verses 2 through 8, Solomon breaks it down so there's no misunderstanding the message. Let's take a look at Solomon's key verse in another translation for clarification: "There is a season (a time appointed) for everything and a time for every delight and event or purpose under heaven" (Eccl. 3:1 AMP).

Considering our schedule enables us to make the *right* commitments for the *right* experience for the *right* purpose. When considering our time, we can be confident of this: God's call to service will complement, not complicate, our schedule. The immeasurably more life is not one of chaotic confusion, like my hummingbird flittering from here to there, doing a lot but accomplishing little. Considering our schedule enables us to make the *right* commitments for the *right* experience for the *right* purpose.

Solomon isn't the only wise man who demonstrated excellent planning. We've journeyed to the center of the Old Testament; let's travel a little further right and go all the way to the beginning of the New Testament. Jesus is the best example of balancing ministry and people.

Jesus healed the blind, lame, and mute yet still had time to attend a wedding with His mother (see John 2:1–11). He taught and fed over five thousand people (see Matt. 14:13–21), then realized He needed to get away to be refreshed (see v. 23). Jesus spent countless hours teaching the people in and around towns and in the temple, but He took time out to have dinner with friends (see Luke 10:38–42). Considering our schedule and accepting the right assignments in the right season will give us room to breathe. Remember, the immeasurably more life should be one adventure after another to be relished, not rushed. A crammed schedule will take away from your experience of the fullness of His presence and magnificent pleasure.

Time is a gift from God, but we don't know when He'll give us our last present. Therefore, we should make the most of the time we are given. Paul spoke to the church at Ephesus about this very subject. He wrote to encourage the young Gentile church to live out their calling as Christians with dignity. (God's Word is so amazing! There's a verse for everything.) "Be very careful, then, how you live—not as unwise but as wise, making the most of every opportunity, because the days are evil" (Eph. 5:15–16).

Grab a pen and underline "making the most of every opportunity." In the Greek, this phrase is represented by the word *exagorazó* (ex-ag-or-ad'-zo).[3] In other translations you will find the word *redeem*, which means "to make wise and sacred use of every opportunity for doing good."[4] Or as David Guzik puts it, "Like a shrewd businessman, buy up opportunities, make the most of every opportunity for Jesus Christ."[5] A shrewd businessman or businesswoman evaluates all prospects and only redeems that which will yield the greatest return. When we make ourselves busy with the wrong service opportunities, we aren't available when the right ones are presented.

Paul said those who make the most of every opportunity are wise. Let's be wise and consider our schedule and pray over every opportunity in order to redeem the right ones. As you pray, think outside the box and be open to changes. Carpool. Watch less TV. Adjust your screen time on your devices. In our busy world, there is so much to consider.

Considering our schedule enables us to make the **right** *commitments for the* **right** *experience for the* **right** *purpose.*

CONSIDER YOUR GIFTS

Researchers Scott Thumma and Warren Bird reported that regardless of the size of the church, 20 percent of the congregants do the work of the church—I totally get this statistic.[6] The sad truth is, our churches are filled with spectators rather than servers. One of the most common excuses for not serving (I've used this often), as stated in an article written by Ed Stetzer and published in *Outreach Magazine*, is that "individuals feel as if they do not have anything significant to offer in ministry. They may believe that they personally are not qualified to serve in a ministry capacity or they might think that only special 'clergy' can truly be involved in God's work."[7]

Have you ever felt like this? Like you aren't gifted and have nothing to offer the kingdom? Often this feeling of uselessness is the result of unbelief or a lack of knowledge of God's Word. Many people don't have a good understanding of spiritual gifts or how to discover what gifts they've been given. They might even feel they aren't worthy of such a gift from God.

Paul referenced spiritual gifts in several different places in the Bible. We'll look at Romans 12:6–8 and 1 Corinthians 12:4–11, 28. Even though we are not specifically told when we receive our spiritual gifts, many Christians believe these gifts are given when we accept Jesus as our Savior. We can be certain that we all receive at least one gift, and some people may receive more than one. "There are different kinds of gifts, but the same Spirit distributes them" (1 Cor. 12:4). No Christian is excluded from the distribution of spiritual gifts. Therefore, we must know how to overcome the feelings of uselessness and unworthiness we might experience from time to time.

The debate of our worthiness can be settled by knowing Scripture: "In his grace, God has given us different gifts for doing certain things well" (Rom. 12:6 NLT), and "Something from the Spirit can be seen in each person" (1 Cor. 12:7 ERV). Through the Spirit, God has imparted a gift, or gifts, to everyone, regardless of background or upbringing. (If you have a pen, underline "everyone.")

Next, we should try to understand more about the different gifts. In the previous paragraphs, I listed places in Scripture that reference spiritual gifts. I've also included a comprehensive list of the gifts and their descriptions in the appendix, where you can also find information about spiritual gifts assessments. Reading the Scripture references and taking a spiritual gifts assessment is a great way to learn about the different spiritual gifts, as well as to determine which gifts God has given you.

Knowing the spiritual gifts and identifying our individual gifts is just the beginning. As part of the body of Christ, the church at large, we have to know the *why* behind our spiritual gifts: "For as in one body we have many members, and the members do not all have the same function, so we, though many, are one body in Christ, and individually members one of another. Having gifts that differ according to the grace given to us, let us use them" (Rom. 12:4–6 ESV).

God gives each of us different gifts so we can help one another. In doing so, we glorify Him. As the body of Christ, we are to work together to build the church, spur one another on to spiritual maturity, and take the gospel of Jesus Christ to the streets. Our gifts are to be used for other people, not our personal gain. In our "me-my-mine" world, this can be hard to grasp. Our natural tendency is to look out for number one, but the disciplines of yes to God and no to self equip us to live in the spiritual rather than the natural. With the greater understanding of our gifts, their role in our lives, and why we have them, it's finally time to *consider.* Perhaps Peter offered the best counsel on doing so: "Based on the gift each one has received, use it to serve others, as good managers of the varied grace of God" (1 Pet. 4:10 HCSB).

In our vigor of discovering our spiritual gifts and the freedom *for* we are enjoying, it's easy to fall into the snare of the activity trap. We are managers of God's gracious gifts; therefore, we must *consider* carefully how we use our gifts. Even when we know our gift and have an opportunity to serve, it doesn't necessarily indicate a green light. Oswald Chambers offered wise words on the subject: "Our ordinary service and reasonable service to God may actually compete against our total surrender to Him. Our reasonable work is based on the following argument which we say to ourselves, 'Remember how useful you are here, and think how much value you would be in that particular type of work.' That attitude chooses our own judgment, instead of Jesus Christ, to be our guide as to where we should go and where we could be used the most."[8]

We must *consider* our people, our schedule, and our gifts, not our own judgment. Leaning on our own judgment can create a world of crowded schedules and neglected people—a place I found myself in a few years ago, when I had to make a tough decision.

In our vigor of discovering our spiritual gifts and the freedom **for** *we are enjoying, it's easy to fall into the snare of the activity trap.*

A person had to be eighteen before they could join the adult choir, and as a teenager, I was counting the days. My voice isn't musically trained, but I can carry a tune. I longed to wear that long green choir robe adorned with a yellow stole. The first Wednesday night after my eighteenth birthday, the choir coordinator gave me my black music folder and an assigned robe. I've loved being part of a choir ever since. Oh, the thrill of walking up into a choir loft, waiting for the first note to be played so the service can start. There's just something about worshipping in a church choir!

Over the decades I have had the privilege of singing in several church choirs and have worn robes of many colors. Serving through singing had been the right place for me. It fit with my people, my schedule, and my gifts … until it didn't. Then it was necessary to pause and consider.

My speaking schedule and writing opportunities had slowly increased. I was serving in church leadership and working part time, and things seemed to be spinning out of control—again. Our home had once again become chaotic because I had become chaotic. My commitments had gotten a hold of me, and I wasn't managing my gifts very well.

My yeses and my noes had beautifully welcomed the freedom of maybe. I was free to sit down and, without reservation, confidently consider all my areas of service. It was clear that even though I could sing, and the opportunity to serve in this way was available, my time doing so had come to an end. To this day I miss it, but I live in the freedom of maybe and know that I made the right decision.

Considering before committing is one of the beautiful themes of freedom that maybe welcomes. We don't have to worry about competition in service or condemnation for not serving. As God directs us, we obey and experience immeasurably more than we can ever think or ask. In saying maybe, we learn to make less of us while making more of Him.

ASK AND IMAGINE

Turn to chapter 10. Before completing a spiritual gifts assessment, write what you *think* your spiritual gifts are. Then after completing the assessment, write out the results. Are you currently using these gifts? If so, how? If not, where are some possible places you could use these gifts?

9

Maybe Confronts What Ifs and a Warning

We have learned to joyfully say yes to God and trust Him in our great adventure of faith. No is getting so much easier to say because we see the picture of God's story and understand that we are little "I's" in the story of the great I AM. We've tasted the freedom that maybe welcomes, and we never want to be caught up in the captivity of activity again. The immeasurably more life *is* truly more than anything we could think of or imagine. However, before we button up this book and bring it to a close, it's important we address the *what ifs* that accompany serving, as well as give a warning to everyone who wants to live with the God of immeasurably more.

Our friend Paul fully lived his life for the One who is able to do "immeasurably more than all we ask," and the apostle proclaimed, "To him be glory in the church and in Christ Jesus throughout all generations, for ever and ever!" (Eph. 3:20–21). Paul served faithfully but faced tough assignments. Let's briefly revisit his hardships.

> I have worked much harder, been in prison more fre-
> quently, been flogged more severely, and been exposed
> to death again and again. Five times I received from
> the Jews the forty lashes minus one. Three times I was
> beaten with rods, once I was pelted with stones, three
> times I was shipwrecked, I spent a night and a day in
> the open sea, I have been constantly on the move. I have
> been in danger from rivers, in danger from bandits, in
> danger from my fellow Jews, in danger from Gentiles;
> in danger in the city, in danger in the country, in danger
> at sea; and in danger from false believers. I have labored
> and toiled and have often gone without sleep; I have
> known hunger and thirst and have often gone without
> food; I have been cold and naked. (2 Cor. 11:23–27)

And he didn't quit. Pause for just a minute to absorb all of this. *What ifs* can take our assignments of service to places we never expected—to experiences of extremes. One extreme could be where everything goes according to plan: people are blessed, they learn about our loving Lord, our relationship with God grows deeper, and we complete our service with no insult or injury. The other end of that spectrum would be experiences like Paul's: people are blessed, God is glorified, your faith grows stronger, but personal suffering comes through the trials of insult and injury.

In one particular incident Paul was stoned and left for dead outside the town of Lystra (Acts 14:19). I can assure you my response to a *what if* situation like this would be different from Paul's reaction, "But as the believers gathered around him, he got up and went back into the town. The next day he left with Barnabas for Derbe" (v. 20 NLT). Paul certainly demonstrated how to finish well.

> **What ifs** *can take our assignments of service*
> *to places we never expected.*

THE WHAT IFS

What if my assignment gets tough?

What if I accepted the wrong assignment?

What if I'm serving for the wrong reason?

The *what ifs* are legitimate concerns. In chapter 8 I shared a couple of examples of service opportunities where the scales of balance were tipped, and adjustments needed to be made. Even when we consider our people, schedule, and gifts, it's possible to end up in a *what if* situation.

The truth is, service can get tough, we might accept a wrong assignment, and we might find ourselves serving for the wrong reason. Regardless of how we start an assignment, every *what if* should be finished well. This isn't a popular concept. The common response to anything that is not going well is to quit. However, the Bible is full of examples of people who finished difficult assignments well.

The world was filled with wickedness, and it troubled God's heart. He decided to restart the population with Noah and his family, so He instructed Noah to build a big boat called an ark (Gen. 6). Noah's family would board the boat and be saved. This assignment took Noah over one hundred years to complete. I would imagine Noah took some ribbing for building an ark for a flood when it had never rained. In one hundred years, Noah had to wonder, *Did I accept the right assignment?* You know the assignment was difficult to complete, yet he finished well. The boat was built, his family was saved, and they repopulated the earth.

> **Regardless of how we start an assignment,**
> **_every_ what if _should be finished well._**

Moses was chosen to lead God's people from Egyptian captivity to the land of promise. Even when the Israelites grumbled about not having water or rich food, Moses continued to lead faithfully. One day, all the complaining got the best of him, and he disobeyed God (Num. 20:6–12). Because of his actions, Moses was not permitted to enter the promised land. Moses could have stormed off and refused to continue to be God's leader, but he didn't. He finished well. And because of Moses's continued devotion, God permitted Moses to see the promised land; then in an act of love, God Himself buried Moses (Deut. 34:4–6).

Paul, our beloved friend Paul, finished well. His assignment was tough. He was beaten, shipwrecked, and put in prison for preaching the gospel of Jesus. The letters to the Ephesians, the Philippians, the Colossians, and Philemon are referred to as the prison epistles because they were written while Paul was in a Roman prison. Try to imagine what our faith lives would be like if Paul hadn't finished well. Oh, the teaching and wisdom we would have missed! His assignments were tough, yet at the close of his life, in his final letter to his beloved Timothy, Paul said, "For I am already being poured out like a drink offering, and the time for my departure is near. I have fought the good fight, I have finished the race, I have kept the faith. Now there is in store for me the crown of righteousness, which the

Lord, the righteous Judge, will award to me on that day—and not only to me, but also to all who have longed for his appearing" (2 Tim. 4:6–8).

Grab your pen and underline "kept the faith." Paul persevered when his assignment was difficult and downright unpleasant. He kept the faith. *Tēréō* (tay-reh'-o) means "to guard from loss or injury by keeping an eye on."[1] This is same word Jesus used when He spoke to the disciples about obedience. "If you love me, keep my commands" (John 14:15). Faith is the Greek word *pistis* (pis'-tis) and is defined by Thayer's lexicon as "conviction or belief respecting man's relationship to God and divine things."[2] Paul guarded his faith, just as Jesus instructed His disciples to guard His commands. His life defined "keeping the faith." Through the violence, death threats, murderous attempts on his life, and prison, he persevered. He truly lived out Acts 20:24: "However, I consider my life worth nothing to me; my only aim is to finish the race and complete the task the Lord Jesus has given me—the task of testifying to the good news of God's grace."

Oh, beautiful! Keeping the faith is not the only aspect to finishing well that Paul demonstrated for us.

Finishing well means that we:

Evidence I'm Finishing Well	Example of Truth
Invest in others to carry on the gospel message. Paul wasn't a one-man show.	"Follow my example, as I follow the example of Christ" (1 Cor. 11:1).
Never grow tired of doing good. Paul did the good and right thing.	"Let us not become weary in doing good, for at the proper time we will reap a harvest if we do not give up" (Gal. 6:9).

Press toward the prize of heaven. Paul endured insults and injury but never wavered.	"I press on toward the goal to win the prize for which God has called me heavenward in Christ Jesus" (Phil. 3:14).
Place confidence in Christ to complete the work. Paul trusted God to complete the work he started.	"For we are God's handiwork, created in Christ Jesus to do good works, which God prepared in advance for us to do" (Eph. 2:10).
Detach from the things of this world. Paul lived a humble life of humble means.	"Let us throw off everything that hinders and the sin that so easily entangles" (Heb. 12:1).
Work to please God, not men. Paul only wanted to please God.	"Work willingly at whatever you do, as though you were working for the Lord rather than for people" (Col. 3:23 NLT).
Stay faithful when others desert us. Paul had many who betrayed him.	"Demas, because he loved this world, has deserted me and has gone to Thessalonica. Crescens has gone to Galatia, and Titus to Dalmatia" (2 Tim. 4:10).

It's important we note that there is some element of risk to serving God. No matter when, where, how, or who you serve, there is chance of physical, emotional, and even spiritual danger. The probability of danger varies from person to person and place to place. Stephen, Andrew, and Peter are all biblical figures who were martyred for their faith in Jesus Christ. There are many examples of modern-day martyrs as well.

In 1956, Jim Elliot and four missionary friends were killed by Auca Indians in Ecuador. In 2010, eight Egyptian Christians were killed after they left a Christmas Mass in Nag Hammadi, Egypt.[3] These deaths are difficult to read about, especially as we are talking about the freedom of saying maybe and the immense joy we have while walking in this freedom. But here's the thing. Each individual I mentioned was serving the God they loved and expanding the gospel of Christ according to their calling. The risk was worth the reward.

When we confront the challenges of *what if*, we do well to remember Paul's wise words when he was afflicted with a "thorn" in his side. Paul prayed three times for God to relieve his pain, his physical problem, but God did not remove it. Our friend's response wasn't to get mad or to say, "I can't serve You because I'm ill." Paul said, "But he said to me, 'My grace is sufficient for you, for my power is made perfect in weakness.' Therefore I will boast all the more gladly about my weaknesses, so that Christ's power may rest on me" (2 Cor. 12:9). Paul accepted the challenge without rejecting servanthood.

We aren't all called to be Pauls. Most of us will not face possible massacres, burning at the stake, or death by execution. However, we will encounter *what if* situations in service. Paul and these others knew the secret to the freedom of maybe. Each lived by depending on the direction of the Holy Spirit *before* they made decisions. I personally didn't know Jim Elliot or any of the others I mentioned who lost their lives for the cause of Christ, but I do know that none of them would have willingly taken the risk for the gospel unless the Spirit had led them. "Since we live by the Spirit, we must also follow the Spirit" (Gal. 5:25 HCSB). The Spirit will never lead us away from God, only toward Him.

The *what if* will come up. The answer to every *what if* is to finish well.

Seek God's direction through prayer, His Word, and other sound Bible-believing, Bible-living friends. Then follow the Spirit's leading:

"Now the Lord is the Spirit, and where the Spirit of the Lord is, there is freedom" (2 Cor. 3:17). We are free, because "it was for freedom that Christ set us free" (Gal. 5:1 NASB). We are free to confront and conquer the *what ifs* and not be worried by the *warning*.

THE WARNING

You might be wondering, *What warning could possibly be associated with this amazing, immeasurably more life and its freedom? If this is the life Jesus died to give, then what could go so wrong that I need a warning?* I know, it doesn't sound right, but hang in there with me.

The sheer joy we have in using our gifts to serve our wonderful Savior, loving Him through our obedience, and living in our new image can actually cause us to lose the plot—we forget the story is about God, not us. It's hard to believe, I know, but we can become "cross I-ed": hyper-aware of the little "I," meaning each of us, rather than staying fixated on the great I AM.

Paul may have sensed this danger when he chose to be identified by his name *Paul*, which means "small," rather than being known as *Saul*, which means "desired." (We discussed this in chapter 1.) Paul seemed to want to embrace humility—to downplay his old identity so he could use his life to glorify the One who is greatest of all.

Our dedication to righteousness can turn into dogmatism.

The cross *I-ed* transition can happen subtly. Without notice, impostors creep in and masquerade as part of our faith, when their sole purpose is to set themselves up *against* our faith. These masked intruders—pride, legalism, and judgmentalism—become part of the story. At first, we want to deny that we have anything to do with them. But if you've ever said phrases like "Yes, the whole worship event was my idea"; "I hope so-and-so was in church today. I'd never skip church like she does"; or "We don't do it that way around here," then let me welcome you to the Cross I-ed Club.

Don't feel bad—you aren't alone. My membership status is current and up to date. A little later in the chapter we will discuss how to manage this membership, but first, let's talk about how the transition from living immeasurably more to cross I-ed living even happens.

The disguised deceivers tiptoe around our commitment to the Word and honoring God. They whisper lies laced with compliments. *You're living the right way now. You need to "help" others to live rightly too.* They crowd our thoughts with messages like *You are important* and *Your opinion matters* and tell us that we've already arrived at the pinnacle of our faith (*No need to work so hard at it anymore*).

With the help of these deceivers, our dedication to righteousness can turn into *dogmatism*. We slowly become like sandpaper—irritating anyone who rubs up against us—rather than behave as gracious bearers of God's fruit.

> *The lines of love are easily blurred. We fall in*
> *love with our own devotion to God instead of*
> *remaining humble in our dedication to God.*

Let's pause to make sure we understand the meaning of *dedicated* and *dogmatic*. I've taken our lesson up a level and visited a thesaurus. The word nerd in me got really excited about this table and all the synonyms ... until I studied the words. Brace yourself.[4]

Word	Definition	Synonyms
Dedicated	"wholly committed to something, as to an ideal"	loyal; steadfast; faithful; earnest; blessed; unwavering; persevering; fervent
Dogmatic	"asserting opinions in a doctrinaire or arrogant manner"	opinionated; bigoted; obstinate; overbearing; arrogant; intolerant; prejudiced

These synonyms are tough—that's why I almost didn't include them. But honestly, seeing them in black and white deepened my understanding of the definitions. My eyes are now wide open, and two things are obvious to me: I want to remain *dedicated* to my relationship to righteousness, and sadly, I've become *dogmatic* in certain areas of life.

The lines of love are easily blurred. We fall in love with our own devotion to God instead of remaining humble in our dedication to God. Our once-pure love becomes proud love. Paul warns us of proud love, "Love is patient, love is kind. It does not envy, it does not boast, it is not proud" (1 Cor. 13:4). This boastful love puffs up with pride, is lofty in legalism, and feels justified in being judge and jury.

MEMBERS OF THE CROSS I-ED CLUB

Sadly, we will all be lifetime members of this club because we live in a fallen world where it's impossible not to sin. However, our membership can move from active to inactive. In order to change our membership status, we have to first be aware of our masked intruders, crusading in our thoughts and confusing the truth with lies. Admitting we've given them access to our life isn't easy, but it's the only way to restore our immeasurably more living. Our source of corrections comes from—you know this—God's Word.

When we recognize the deceivers, we must return to the disciplines, open our Bible, and renew our minds with truth. The blurred lines of love will once again become clear as the light of God's Word reveals the impostors and offers correction to redirect our actions.

The Puff of Pride

As GotQuestions.org puts it, "Pride is essentially self-worship."[5] Again, another collection of words that are hard to swallow. Without keeping our eyes fixed on Jesus, the Author and Perfecter of our faith (see Heb. 12:2), we will fall for self-worship as fast as a rock sinks in water. We can't afford to take our eyes off Him for one single second. Pride takes credit instead of giving credit. Pride is more concerned about being recognized than giving recognition to God or anyone else. Pride is life without humility, and a life without humility will lead to destruction. "Pride goes before destruction" (Prov. 16:18). It destroys the intimacy with God that we worked so hard to create. If we don't guard ourselves against this masked invader, we will eventually sit on the throne of conceit.

God is not a fan of arrogance. In fact, He has strong opinions on the subject. "To fear the LORD is to hate evil; I hate pride and arrogance, evil behavior and perverse speech" (Prov. 8:13). And just in case you are wondering, yes, *hate* means exactly what you think it means: "to dislike intensely or passionately; feel extreme aversion for or extreme hostility toward."[6] It's difficult to use the word *hate* in the same sentence with *God*, isn't it? God is love. God saves. God forgives. God gives grace—and yes, God hates.

God has an aversion to anything elevated above Him. He says, "How can I let myself be defamed? I will not yield my glory to another" (Isa. 48:11). "I am the LORD; that is my name! I will not yield my glory to another or my praise to idols" (42:8). When we become arrogant about what we think we know to be right, we put distance between ourselves and others—and between us and God. How can we take pride in any knowledge we have when everything we have comes from Him? "What are you so puffed up about? What do you have that God hasn't given you? And if all you have is from God, why act as though you are so great, and as though you have accomplished something on your own?" (1 Cor. 4:7 TLB).

God has an aversion to anything elevated above Him.

The only way to take the puff out of pride is to live a life of humility. Our life is a classroom. If we are having trouble with our dethroning, God will step in and help us with some real-time teaching. Sometimes we need a lesson in humility, and falling from our own throne is the only way to learn. And falling hurts, friends—especially when you go down in front of people thirty years younger than you.

When my daughter was a junior, we visited many prospective colleges. Nothing tells a woman of a certain age "You're old" like walking onto a college campus. In an effort to fight that aging feeling, I selected a youthful outfit to wear, pending my daughter's approval, of course. We ladies want to look stylish while remembering we *are not* in our late teens or early twenties. Blaire approved of my longer "man shirt" (from my hubby's closet), leggings, and tall boots. The outfit was pulled together with a multicolor scarf. I will admit, I was feeling tastefully young.

On this visit I had two girls with me: my daughter and her best friend. They spent the night in the dorms and the morning going to classes and sessions just for them. We love Mexican food, so for lunch I took them to a local restaurant. The food was amazing, and I loved every second with my girls. We all made a stop at the ladies' room before returning to campus.

We're friends, right? So, we can speak candidly, right? When we enter the bathroom stall, we have two choices: to line or to hover. The choice is a personal decision for every woman, and it might vary from bathroom to bathroom. On this visit I chose to line. After completing my business, I tucked, flushed, and washed, then met the girls in the car. Let me insert: at this point I was feeling quite cute and really enjoying myself with my young-adult girls. After dropping them off at their building, I headed to the student union (the place where the students—many, many students—gather to hang out) to return the sleeping mats the girls had borrowed.

Still full of joy and fun, I retrieved the mats from the trunk of the car. Energetically I raced up the outside stairs *full of students*, walked through the lobby *full of students*, went downstairs to return the mats, and then went back upstairs through the lobby *full of students* to the office where I was to meet with financial advisers.

Feeling a little breathless and tousled, I straightened my cute "man shirt" as I sat down—only to discover an accessory I had not fashioned with my outfit. *Yes.* Yes indeed, the very paper I had used to line my toilet seat was tucked into my leggings. Will you pause (after you stop laughing) to fellowship in my suffering? Through the restaurant, across the parking lot, up the stairs, through the lobby, down the stairs, back up the stairs, through the lobby again, the white stream of single-ply paper had waved to everyone behind me.

If prancing around a college campus with toilet paper hanging out of your pants doesn't dethrone you, I'm not sure what will.

(Feel free to take a moment to regain your composure before continuing.)

Lofty in Legalism

For most of my life I wasn't a fan of rules. It's been said that I would argue with a fence post to get my way. Manipulation was my game. Every rule could be *bent*, and every boundary could be moved; I just had to use my words creatively to move or bend things in my direction. This is not something I am particularly proud of, but this was a way of life for me from a very young age.

My mother is one of those women whose shoes, belt, and bag all match. Her lipstick and liner have always been perfectly applied. She has always been a beautiful woman who followed all the proper dress etiquette, like the unwritten rule about wearing dresses to church. Whether it was Sunday morning church, Sunday evening Training Union (nowadays we call it "discipleship classes"), or missions on Wednesday, I wore a dress to church.

This didn't bother me until I was old enough to notice that my girlfriends were allowed to wear pants to church on Wednesday nights. It was a more casual setting. We played games and did crafts, so it made sense that pants would be an option. So I prepared my case for wearing pants and confidently took it to my mother. She listened (which says a lot) but respectfully denied my request. Each week, I walked into my missions class wearing a dress, while all the other girls donned the latest in pant fashion. I was so envious and determined to get my mother to change her mind.

Beware the creative genius of a strong-willed middle school girl. It took some time, but eventually I came up with another plan to present to my mother.

"Momma, I know that I can't wear pants every week, but can I wear pants once a month?" Pretty good, huh? After weeks of nonstop harassing, she finally gave in. Bam—*rule bent.* But the bent rule only satisfied me for a short while; I wanted more. Cleverly, I manipulated her by asking her to allow me to wear pants multiple times a month if I skipped wearing pants in future months to repay the debt. Finally, I wore my mother down until the borrowing from other months meant I was wearing pants every week just like the other girls. Bam—*boundary moved.*

Unfortunately, I carried this bend-and-move idea into my obedience with God. I didn't really like His boundaries at first. But what I realized was that, though I might try to bend His rules to suit me, God would never be moved, and His boundaries were set with good reason. They were there for my safety and to help me grow. Over time, I began to love the security of His limitations. They gave me confidence, because I knew exactly what was expected of me as one of His children.

Obedience is essential in our relationship with God, but legalism and knowledge of the Word should never replace love.

However, without my realizing it, this confidence turned into arrogance. I appointed myself the Word and Doctrine police. My policing was overbearing and intolerant. Rather than attracting others to Jesus with love and joy, I repelled them with finger pointing and correction. It sickens me now to think of those I turned away from Jesus during my legalistic phase.

To lift the lofty attitude of legalism, we have to merge truth with mercy. Without mercy, we tear each other down instead of build each other up. Paul consistently talked about building up the body of Christ. In his letter to the church of Ephesus, he wrote, "Instead, speaking the truth in love, we will grow to become in every respect the mature body of him who is the head, that is, Christ. From him the whole body, joined and held together by every supporting ligament, grows and builds itself up in love, as each part does its work" (Eph. 4:15–16). Obedience is essential in our relationship with God, but legalism and knowledge of the Word should never replace love. "But while knowledge makes us feel important, it is love that strengthens the church. Anyone who claims to know all the answers doesn't really know very much" (1 Cor. 8:1–2 NLT). "Let love be your highest goal" (14:1 NLT).

Justified in Being Judge and Jury

Maybe pride and legalism aren't the deceivers whispering in your ear. Perhaps instead you've elected yourself judge and jury to all those who seemingly fall short of the holy standards of the Word and how you determine they should be lived. I've gotten caught up in such a superiority complex too.

It's so easy to drive around in our community, shop in our local stores, attend church services on Sunday, and wrestle with a "Hmm. I'm glad I'm not like that" or "I certainly have never had to face that demon" attitude. Paul warns us about selectively placing judgment on others when he teaches about God's wrath on humanity and the depravity of man. He says people have become filled with every kind of wickedness, evil, greed, and depravity. He further calls out envy, murder, strife, deceit, and malice, and he warns of gossips, slanderers, God haters, the insolent, arrogant people, and braggarts (see Rom. 1:29–30). Then he says something that should rattle anyone going toe to toe with their self: "'Well,' you may be saying, 'what terrible people you have been talking about!' But wait a minute! You are just as bad. When you say they are wicked and should be punished, you are talking about yourselves, for you do these very same things" (Rom. 2:1 TLB). Ouch! That was painful, wasn't it?

So then, how do we refrain from judging? The writer of Hebrews offers very wise counsel on the matter: "We should think about each other to see how we can encourage each other to show love and do good works. We must not quit meeting together, as some are doing. No, we need to keep on encouraging each other. This becomes more and more important as you see the Day getting closer" (Heb. 10:24–25 ERV). Judgment is unmasked when it is replaced with benevolence. Living with the God of immeasurably more means that we consider others first. Let's hear what two immeasurably more experts, Jesus and Paul, had to say about this.

> Don't be interested only in your own life, but care about the lives of others too. (Phil. 2:4 ERV)

> God has chosen you and made you his holy people. He loves you. So your new life should be like this:

Show mercy to others. Be kind, humble, gentle, and patient. (Col. 3:12 ERV)

All people will know that you are my followers if you love each other. (John 13:35 ERV)

He answered, "If you have two shirts, share with someone who does not have one. If you have food, share that too." (Luke 3:11 ERV)

Considering the needs of others and concentrating on showing them grace is the way to get out of the trap of being judgmental. It's hard to judge someone if you are busy trying to love them.

Judgment is unmasked when it is replaced with benevolence.

I hope you can see now why I included the warning to not get cross I-ed. In fact, I needed to hear it for myself as much, if not more, than I needed to give it to you. I still have to watch out every day. I have to remind myself that our dogmatism can temporarily derail our dedication. But God always welcomes us back. Acknowledging and confessing our sin will restore our relationship with our loving Father. Though we may be led astray by the impostors of pride, legalism, and judgment, we can never be snatched away. Jesus made this promise: "I give them eternal life, and they shall never perish; no one will snatch them out of my hand" (John 10:28). Turning from the plot stealers, we can recognize and embrace the true by-products of our faith.

Our devotion produces gratitude, praise, and worship. Our yeses and noes welcome a life of freedom in Christ that we could only imagine. A life that has the astounding privilege of experiencing the indwelling of God Himself, through His Spirit living in us. "For the Lord is the Spirit, and wherever the Spirit of the Lord is, there is freedom" (2 Cor. 3:17 NLT). His Word instructs us. His Spirit directs us. He gives boundless love, limitless grace, and endless mercy. Such goodness can't be contained. We are a living, breathing testimony to His magnificent affection for creation. The realization fills our hearts with indebtedness, ignites compulsory praise, and produces songs of worship that fall from our lips and tears of gratitude that spill from our eyes. When this phenomenon consumes us, and we live in tandem with the heartbeat of God, we rejoice in playing a supportive role in the story of the One. We are uninhibited to live out all our days making much of Him.

It's hard to judge someone if you are busy trying to love them.

MUCH OF HIM

How do we wrap up such an amazing journey together? This is probably the hardest part of writing a book. The final word. The last hurrah. I wish I could look each of you in the eyes and cup your beautiful face in my hand and lean close so you can hear the desperation in my voice. Oh, don't dismiss the message of *Yes, No, and Maybe*. If you do, you will miss the fullness of the life Jesus died to give you.

When we make much of Him, by default we make less of us.

If I could take your face in my hand, and look in your bright eyes, I'd say in an urgent tone, "Don't meet Jesus with any regrets. Run hard after Him. His Word is life. His Spirit is truth. His ways are trustworthy. He's the sweetest, kindest, most generous Man who will ever love you. He's funny, and fun to hang around with. The life you've always wanted is waiting for you, and when you discover it, make much of Him."

In September 2004, Steven Curtis Chapman released another song that challenged and changed my life. "Much of You" encapsulates the entire message of our purpose and is the correct response to the incredible honor of living with the God of immeasurably more. It's my life's theme. When we make much of Him, by default we make less of us. The song talks about looking at all the wonder of the mountains and the sky and realizing that "I'm just a whisper, and You are the thunder." Then the chorus declares this: "I give You my life / Take and let it be used / To make much of You."

The first time I heard "Much of You," I was sitting on a bench, staring at the vastness of the ocean while the afternoon sun kissed my face. The song was released as I was on the cusp of figuring out that the story wasn't about me, my happiness, or anything I could accomplish. The chasing hard after God, spending time with Jesus each morning, and yielding to the work of His Word through the power of the Holy Spirit weren't about making my life better for me, but to make my life an offering for Him.

Learning the pure joy of pouring myself out as an offering to Him hasn't come without its trials, temptations, and tests. Pursuing the immeasurably more life isn't for the faint of faith. I guess that's why so few Christians experience it and are content sitting in church each Sunday, asking the same question Melvin asked, "Is this as good as it gets?" The pains of the hard work pale in comparison to the richness of calling on God, Abba, and experiencing the thrill of participating in His plan to expand His kingdom and the peace of knowing that nothing will touch you unless it first passes through His hand.

Don't miss it, my sweet amazing friend! Not one single minute of it!

Let's finish where we started. Paul's prayer for his friends at the church in Ephesus is my prayer for you.

> When I think of the wisdom and scope of his plan, I fall down on my knees and pray to the Father of all the great family of God—some of them already in heaven and some down here on earth—that out of his glorious, unlimited resources he will give you the mighty inner strengthening of his Holy Spirit. And I pray that Christ will be more and more at home in your hearts, living within you as you trust in him. May your roots go down deep into the soil of God's marvelous love; and may you be able to feel and understand, as all God's children should, how long, how wide, how deep, and how high his love really is; and to experience this love for yourselves, though it is so great that you will never see the end of it or fully know or understand it. And so at last you will be filled up with God himself.
>
> Now glory be to God, who by his mighty power at work within us is able to do far more than we would ever dare to ask or even dream of—infinitely beyond

our highest prayers, desires, thoughts, or hopes. May he be given glory forever and ever through endless ages because of his master plan of salvation for the Church through Jesus Christ. (Eph. 3:14–21 TLB)

ONE LAST THOUGHT

And about the thirteen words … my Scott says to tell you that, today, our home is a place he *loves* to come to.

ASK AND IMAGINE

What areas of your devotion to God have become dogmatic? What has God taught you about finishing well?

10

My Immeasurably More Life

INTRODUCTION

Make an honest list of the "uns" in your life. Then draw a line through each of them. Write out the new superabundantly scripts we created when studying Ephesians 3:20.

_____

_____

_____

_____

_____

_____

_____

_____

_____

_____

CHAPTER 1

Write about your Damascus road experience. End the section by listing every one of your new names. When did your sin meet Jesus's salvation? What is your new name?

_____

_____

_____

_____

_____

_____

_____

_____

_____

_____

_____

_____

_____

_____

_____

_____

_____

_____

_____

_____

_____

_____

_____

CHAPTER 2

With which obstacle do you most struggle? Finding your *want to*: the obstacle of self? Finding your willpower: the obstacle of sin? Or finding your worth: the obstacle of shame? What part of your life is affected most by this struggle? Moving forward, how will you overcome this obstacle?

CHAPTER 3

What are some of your current obsessions? Paul's two-part instruction in Romans 12:2 is challenging. **Instruction 1: Don't copy what the world is doing.** How are you currently copying the world? **Instruction 2: Let God transform the way you think.** What adjustments can you make in your life to allow God to begin the transformation process in you?

CHAPTER 4

What will peeling back the layers of the onion reveal in your life? Examine Galatians 5:22–23 carefully. "But the fruit of the Spirit is love, joy, peace, forbearance, kindness, goodness, faithfulness, gentleness and self-control. Against such things there is no law." What fruit shines in your life? What fruit needs to grow?

_____

_____

_____

_____

_____

_____

_____

_____

_____

_____

_____

_____

_____

_____

_____

_____

_____

_____

_____

CHAPTER 5

A is for Analyze. Spend some time with the concealers.

Strongholds: a well-fortified place; fortress; a defensible place. A place of a spiritual battle.
Self-Centeredness: moderate concern with one's own interests and well-being; self-love or egotism.
Self-Sufficiency: having extreme confidence in one's own resources, powers, etc.

Which concealers are the greatest struggle for you? Why?

_____

_____

_____

_____

_____

_____

_____

_____

_____

_____

_____

_____

_____

CHAPTER 6

In 2 Timothy 3:16–17 (NASB) we read: "All Scripture is inspired by God and profitable for teaching, for reproof, for correction, for training in righteousness; so that the man of God may be adequate, equipped for every good work." How do you respond to the Spirit's work in your life?

Teaching: giving instruction
Reproof: reproachment or conviction
Correction: restoration to the proper condition
Training: instructing someone to reach maturity

_____

_____

_____

_____

_____

_____

_____

_____

_____

_____

_____

_____

_____

CHAPTER 7

What most excites you about freedom *for*: radical living, lavish loving, or generous giving? Why? In what ways (if any) are you already demonstrating these in your life?

CHAPTER 8

Before completing a spiritual gifts assessment, write what you *think* your spiritual gifts are. Then after completing the assessment, write out the results. Are you currently using these gifts? If so, how? If not, where are some possible places you could use these gifts?

_____

_____

_____

_____

_____

_____

_____

_____

_____

_____

_____

_____

_____

_____

_____

_____

_____

_____

CHAPTER 9

What areas of your devotion to God have become dogmatic? What has God taught you about finishing well?

Epilogue

I was at the end of my rope and desperately wanted God to fix my fractured home. I believed if He would just fix my husband, my life would be absolutely perfect, just the way I dreamed. Little did I know that in fixing my fractured home, God would have to repair a flawed me.

In an attempt to escape the reality of my lonely, and what I believed to be an unfulfilled, day-to-day life, I packed my suitcase, gathered all my "uns," and headed to a women's conference with several ladies from my Bible study group. The goal: escape my reality. My desperation for escape was so great, I willingly drove eight hours to attend this event. It was my intention to make my time away as selfish as possible: eating where and what *I* wanted to eat, sleeping where and as long as *I* wanted to sleep. The weekend was going to be all about me, and if I happened to learn something new about Jesus, that would be fine. If not, well, that was fine too. Little did I know that my *escape* was God's plan to have a one-on-one *encounter* with me in a church full of 2,500 women.

We walked into this Church of Christ to begin session one, and everything seemed "normal" to this Southern Baptist girl, until the praise and worship started. It seemed as if the church was divided into two groups: those who were demonstrative in their worship and those who were not. I was on the "not" side. As I sang the unfamiliar worship songs, I observed. I watched the others sing. They looked different; their hands were raised, and their faces were stained with tears. They worshipped with such authenticity. It was perplexing, but I was there to *escape*, not to dissect the worship display of some ladies I didn't know.

The first session ended, and the party was on. We headed to a grown-up restaurant to eat. I felt like a rebel eating so late, and there wasn't a child in sight. Oh, the bliss! I ordered from the grown-up menu. After dinner we went back to the hotel, where we stayed up late talking, then rose at early dark-thirty to get back to the church for the remainder of the conference.

As the praise and worship time began in session two, I noticed a strange phenomenon. It seemed as if some of the demonstrative worshippers were sitting on the "not" side of the sanctuary. Or had something spiritual happened overnight to stir the "not" hearts? I actually found myself smiling as I sang, and I began moving ever so slightly to the beat of the music. But nothing too crazy—after all, I was a Baptist girl. (You know you're smiling.) Could it be that my heart was softening? We heard more wonderful Bible teaching, then session two drew to a close.

Later that day as the music began to play to start session three, the two groups were completely mixed. God was working to unite and change hearts, and He was starting with me. I sang the songs as if I had known them my whole life. This traditional, nondemonstrating Southern Baptist girl actually raised her hands—*just a little bit*. No one could believe the transformation that had taken place among us. At the close of session three, the teacher offered an invitation to come forward and pray, or pray to receive Christ as Savior. Many walked forward—some alone, some in pairs. The Holy Spirit was hard at work.

Before the invitation time closed, the worship leader led one final song, "We Will Dance." In the middle of the song, he stopped and asked if anyone felt led to come to the stage and dance. Let me tell you, in my world, dance and church did not go together. I held my breath in anticipation of what was about to happen. When the music continued, several women flooded the stage and danced. Tears puddled and poured from my eyes. Never had I witnessed such a moving display of worship. It was truly breathtaking.

Then the music stopped. I quickly suppressed the emotions that stirred my heart and later turned on the humor for the ride home.

For days after returning home from the conference, I wrestled with a heavy heart and troubled spirit. My home was a wreck; the escape didn't fix anything. In fact, it complicated things even more. What was wrong with me?

I reflected on the in-depth teaching and powerful, authentic worship I had experienced at the conference. The Holy Spirit led me in the end to myself, to finally resolve the reason for my emotional mess. The root of my troubled spirit was jealousy. I was jealous of the women at the conference. They held and marked in their Bibles like they were familiar with the content. They worshipped with a reverence and awe that said, "Oh, yes, that's my God!" They worshipped Him as if they had experienced firsthand His mercy, love, grace, and forgiveness. Their love for Him could not be contained. Right then and there, I determined to know God and His Word like they did, so I would worship Him like they did. Jeremiah 29:13 became my theme, and it did not disappoint: "You will seek and find me when you seek me with all your heart."

I sought Him and I found Him.

THE REST OF THE STORY

My life transformation began at that women's conference and with the thirteen words. Ironically God brought me back to another conference led by the same Bible teacher almost eight years later. The scenario was quite different this time, though. I went to the first conference to *escape* the reality of my unfulfilled life; this time I was going to *experience* Jesus. My fractured home wasn't completely fixed, but my eyes were completely fixed on God, and my life had been changed by His Word. With Bible in tow and a heart prepared to hear from the Lord, I boarded a plane to Baltimore.

The conference spanned five days. The ten teaching sessions were recorded for the Bible teacher's upcoming in-depth Bible study. The teaching times were intense, but I loved every minute of them. The sanctuary was filled with women hungry for truth and with the rhythm of Bible pages turning back and forth. The uplifting worship music took us to the heights of heaven's gates. Different nations, tribes, and tongues praising our great God in beautiful harmony. It was heaven on earth.

As wonderful as the heaven-on-earth experience was, on the fifth day we were all ready to return home to our families, none more so than our fearless leader. She had unselfishly poured herself out as a beautiful sacrifice to the Lord. Everyone was moved by her authenticity, as well as her commitment to teaching the truth with meaning and excellence. Applause filled the room in appreciation at the close of the final session. As we turned to leave, we heard her voice as she returned to the stage. A hush fell over the room. "We need to sing one more song. I don't know why, but we do."

The worship leader did not miss a beat. He took her cue and asked the sound tech to play the second-to-last track on the last CD. To this day, I am not sure if he knew the title to the track, but God did.

Standing in the balcony, I heard and recognized the song immediately. This song had become part of my heart over the previous eight years. On my personal copy this track was worn out with skips. My mind flashed back to the first time I heard this song and watched the women dance on stage. It wasn't a song randomly selected—it was selected for me by my Daddy: "We Will Dance."

I was overwhelmed by the moment. He had brought me full circle. What had left me bewildered eight years earlier now held me captive. God intimately met me in a crowd of several thousand women. I was no longer jealous, because I was one of *those* women. On that day, I adored and worshipped Him. My firsthand experience with His mercy, love, grace, and forgiveness made it possible to dance with Him, and I didn't care who was watching.

One day, we will all dance before Him. I can't wait to meet you there.

"Oh, we will dance on the streets that are golden, the glorious bride and the great Son of Man. Let every tongue and tribe and nation rejoice in the song of the Lamb."[1]

Let's serve Him, and each other, until we see Him.

Appendix

Spiritual Gifts Assessment

Give each statement a score of 1, 2, 3, 4, or 5; with 5 meaning it sounds a lot like you and 1 meaning it's really not your cup of tea. When you're finished ranking all the statements, turn to the scoring key and follow the instructions to add up your scores. See which gifts produce the highest scores for you. For more about spiritual gifts, read Romans 12:6–8; 1 Corinthians 12; Ephesians 4:11–13; and 1 Peter 4:8–11.

1.		I love the idea of being sent to other cultures to do ministry.
2.		My favorite thing in the world is to proclaim to people the written Word of God.
3.		It fills me with endless joy when I can tell people about Jesus and see them come to faith in Him.
4.		I rise up like a mama bear when I see someone heading toward spiritual shipwreck.

5.		I absolutely love teaching and explaining to others the truths and joys of God.
6.		I love to say something that puts the wind back in the sails of someone who was discouraged.
7.		I feel most like I've truly worshipped God when I've received a new insight about His character or His Word.
8.		Whenever I'm in conversation with unbelievers, ideas of what to say just pop into my mind, and they end up being the perfect things to have said.
9.		The idea of personally helping a minister (or someone doing the work of God) be freed up from menial labor to do God's work gives me great joy.
10.		I love to bring the stranger or traveler into my home—especially if the person can't return the favor.
11.		It thrills my soul when I can give money or resources to others, so they will be strengthened.
12.		I love planning and organizing so that people are treated fairly and systems operate efficiently.
13.		When I say "How can I help?" I'm not just being nice—I'm actually asking for what the most urgent needs are, so I can work to supply them.
14.		Once I see that God wants something done, I will press on and pray with authority until it comes to pass.
15.		I instantly recognize it when what someone is saying is false or when people's words don't line up with their lives.

16.		The idea of going where people have never heard about Jesus, and maybe even planting a church, is incredibly appealing to me.
17.		I can detect false teaching a mile away, even when others don't seem to hear it.
18.		I love presenting Christ to people in such a way that they have to get off the fence and make a decision about their faith.
19.		I see potential in people that they don't even see in themselves, and I love calling it out in them.
20.		I can often see what God wants done, and then I strike off to make it happen, thanking Him for it, as if it's already in place.
21.		I am unusually inspired by the story of Barnabas selling his land and giving all the proceeds to the church.
22.		I can instantly tell when the group's conversation is getting off point, and I can gently bring it back to the main topic.
23.		It propels me to action when I hear that a servant of God is being hindered in gospel work because of mundane duties or obligations.
24.		I love opening my home to people in need.
25.		It gives me a special thrill when I suddenly see a new principle in God's Word.

26.		It especially bothers me when someone gives "be warmed and filled" words only and doesn't actually do something to ease someone's suffering.
27.		If I could spend my days doing nothing but proclaiming the Word of God to people, I would be overjoyed.
28.		It thrills me to no end when something I say causes someone to move into more growth and sustenance in the Lord.
29.		People tell me I have an uncanny ability to say things so clearly that they instantly understand even very difficult concepts.
30.		When faced with dilemmas that others find baffling, oftentimes a biblical principle will come to my mind and ends up solving the problem perfectly.
31.		When I know God wants a thing done, I go boldly before His throne, pleading with authority for Him to bring it to pass.
32.		It lights my fires to take my understanding of any topic I'm passionate about and communicate it to others.
33.		I love to be the one who makes copies or runs errands or does anything else that allows someone to concentrate on doing the work of the kingdom.
34.		My kindness to others in need is so great that some have said I'm too soft hearted.

35.		I deeply resonate with any story of someone rising up to stand in the gap for the little ones who believe in God, especially when spiritual harm was going to come to them.
36.		I have a special talent for unmasking Satan's trickery, detecting false teaching, and ferreting out false teachers.
37.		I find I am so competent in debating with unbelievers that I am sometimes invited to defend the gospel before others.
38.		Because correct giving is done in secret, and because I love to give like that, I feel especially troubled when people try to get attention for giving to the church or other ministries.
39.		I often find that I have understood deep things about God's character or ways that have never occurred to many of those around me.
40.		I receive great personal delight when I get to play host for any gathering of people.
41.		I get a deep joy from setting goals, making plans, and motivating people to carry them out.
42.		The idea of being sent out and commissioned to gospel work thrills me like nothing else.
43.		When I preach in the Lord's name, power flows out and people are changed.
44.		I find that even when I consider my presentation of the gospel to have been lackluster, the Spirit nevertheless blesses and draws people to conversion.

45.		When I speak to people, they gain hope and new strength to stride out again.
46.		One of my greatest delights is receiving special insights from God about His character, His plan, and His Word.
47.		It thrills me to no end to be able to give financially to someone, especially when my gift is going to further the kingdom.
48.		It absolutely lights my fires to offer guidance to people that steers them toward spiritual health and/or away from spiritual harm.
49.		When I teach or explain something, I sense that God is making the communication not only very clear but also deeply impactful for the listeners.
50.		When I become convinced that God wants a thing done, I march to God's throne with prayer and effort until God's plan for that thing takes form on the earth.
51.		Nothing thrills my soul more than telling someone about the unsearchable riches available in Christ if that person will only come to Him in faith.
52.		When faced with a baffling dilemma or when challenged about my faith, I seem to always receive from God the right biblical principle to apply or the perfect thing to say.
53.		I love to encourage people who are down, and if something I say gives them new strength to face their struggles, I feel the pleasure of God.

54.		If I could do anything in the world, I would travel to another culture, learn another language, embrace the people and their customs, and win as many as possible for the kingdom.
55.		It moves me to action when I see a servant of the gospel burdened with lesser tasks, and I am so gratified when I can take those off that person so that the real work can move forward.
56.		I seem to have an unusual ability to sense when someone's doctrine doesn't line up with truth, and I can rest easy only when that discord is resolved.
57.		My joy is to bring efficiency, organization, and humility into a system so that the plans and efforts to advance God's kingdom can operate smoothly.
58.		I love bringing people into my home, especially people in need or in distress, and I feel it is my special ministry to do so.
59.		I often change my schedule and go far out of my way to do an act of kindness for someone who is suffering, and it thrills my soul to do so.
60.		What is most needed in almost any situation or crisis is the presentation of the Word of God and its application for correction.

SCORING KEY

Add your scores from the relevant question numbers, as shown below, to get your total score for each gift. Share your scores with an account-ability partner, a friend, or a member of your Bible study group. What do your scores tell you? Were you surprised at all by your results? If you are not already involved in serving your local church, what areas might appeal to you most, based on your Spiritual Gifts Assessment? Take time to pray and consider where God might be guiding you to serve as part of the body of Christ.

Total	Gift	Add Questions
	Apostleship	1, 16, 42, 54
	Prophecy	2, 27, 43, 60
	Evangelism	3, 18, 44, 51
	Shepherding	4, 28, 35, 48
	Teaching	5, 29, 32, 49
	Exhortation	6, 19, 45, 53
	Word of Knowledge	7, 25, 39, 46
	Word of Wisdom	8, 30, 37, 52
	Helps	9, 23, 33, 55
	Hospitality	10, 24, 40, 58
	Giving	11, 21, 38, 47
	Government	12, 22, 41, 57
	Mercy	13, 26, 34, 59
	Faith	14, 20, 31, 50
	Discernment	15, 17, 36, 56

Notes

INTRODUCTION

1. Bible Hub, s.v. "*huper*," accessed May 24, 2018, http://biblehub.com/greek /5228.htm.

2. Bible Hub, s.v. "*perissos*," accessed May 24, 2018, http://biblehub.com/greek /4053.htm.

CHAPTER 1: OBEDIENCE: OUR FIRST YES

1. Bible Hub, s.v. "*sótéria*," accessed May 25, 2018, http://biblehub.com/greek /4991.htm.

2. Bible Hub, s.v. "*pisteuó*," accessed May 25, 2018, http://www.biblehub.com/greek /4100.htm.

3. Quency E. Wallace, "The Early Life and Background of Paul the Apostle," *American Journal of Biblical Theology*, 2002, www.biblicaltheology.com/Research /WallaceQ01.html.

4. Alexander Maclaren, "Why Saul Became Paul," Bible Hub, accessed May 25, 2018, http://biblehub.com/library/maclaren/expositions_of_holy_scripture _the_acts/why_saul_became_paul.htm.

5. Casting Crowns, "East to West," *The Altar and the Door*, Beach Street, 2007.

6. Bible Hub, s.v. "*kurios*," accessed May 25, 2018, http://biblehub.com/str/greek /2962.htm.

7. Bible Hub, s.v. "*Iésous*," accessed May 25, 2018, http://biblehub.com/greek/ 2424.htm.

CHAPTER 3: OBSESSION OF YES

1. Dictionary.com, s.v. "obsession," accessed May 25, 2018, www.dictionary.com /browse/obsession?s=t.

2. Steven Curtis Chapman, "Magnificent Obsession," *Declaration*, Sparrow Records, 2001.

3. Dictionary.com, s.v. "transformation," accessed May 25, 2018, www.dictionary .com/browse/transformation?s=t.

CHAPTER 4: NO TO SELF: ACCEPTING MY NEW IMAGE

1. Dictionary.com, s.v. "created," accessed May 30, 2018, www.dictionary.com /browse/created?s=t.

2. StudyLight.org, s.v. "*agapé*," accessed May 30, 2018, www.studylight.org/lexicons /greek/26.html.

3. William Barclay, *New Testament Words* (London: Westminster Press, 1974), 21.

4. StudyLight.org, s.v. "*chara*," accessed May 30, 2018, www.studylight.org/lexicons /greek/5479.html.

5. Charles H. Spurgeon, "The Fruit of the Spirit: Joy," Answers in Genesis, November 20, 2014, https://answersingenesis.org/education/ spurgeon-sermons/1582-the-fruit-of-the-spirit-joy/.

6. StudyLight.org, s.v. "*eiréné*," accessed May 30, 2018, www.studylight.org/lexicons /greek/1515.html.

7. StudyLight.org, s.v. "*eiréné*," *William Barclay's Daily Study Bible*, accessed May 30, 2018, www.studylight.org/commentaries/dsb/galatians-5.html.

8. Bible Hub, s.v. "*makrothumia*," accessed May 30, 2018, http://biblehub.com/greek /3115.htm.

9. Bible Hub, s.v. "*chréstotés*," accessed May 30, 2018, http://biblehub.com/greek /5544.htm.

10. Bible Hub, s.v. "*agathosune*," accessed May 30, 2018, http://biblehub.com/greek /19.htm.

11. Bible Hub, s.v. "*pistis*," accessed May 30, 2018, http://biblehub.com/greek /4102.htm.

12. StudyLight.org, "Commentary on Galatians," *Martin Luther's Commentary*, accessed May 30, 2018, www.studylight.org/commentaries/mlg/galatians -5.html16.

13. Bible Hub, s.v. "*praotés*," accessed May 30, 2018, http://biblehub.com/greek /4236.htm.

14. Leon Morris, *Galatians: Paul's Charter of Christian Freedom* (Downers Grove, IL: InterVarsity, 1996), https://enduringword.com/bible-commentary/galatians-5/.

15. StudyLight.org, s.v. "*enkráteia*," accessed May 30, 2018, www.studylight.org /lexicons/greek/1466.html.

16. David Guzik, "Galatians 5: Standing Fast in the Liberty of Jesus," Enduring Word, accessed May 30, 2018, https://enduringword.com/bible-commentary /galatians-5/.

17. Knowing Jesus, s.v. "*meno*," accessed May 30, 2018, https://bible.knowing-jesus .com/strongs/G3306.

18. Bible Hub, s.v. "*karpós*," accessed May 30, 2018, http://biblehub.com/ greek/2590.htm.

CHAPTER 5: NO TO SELF: ANALYZING WHAT CONCEALS MY IMAGE

1. Louie Giglio, *I Am Not but I Know I AM: Welcome to the Story of God* (Colorado Springs: Multnomah, 2005), 38–39.

2. Dictionary.com, s.v. "stronghold," "self-centered," "self-sufficient," accessed May 31, 2018, www.dictionary.com/browse/stronghold?s=t; www.dictionary.com /browse/self-centered?s=t; www.dictionary.com/browse/self-sufficiency?s=ts. Bible Hub, s.v. "*dunamis*," "*agapé*," "*sóphronismos*," accessed May 31, 2018, http://biblehub.com/greek/1411.htm; http://biblehub.com/greek/26.htm; http://biblehub.com/greek/4995.htm.

CHAPTER 6: NO TO SELF: ADJUSTING TO MY NEW IMAGE

1. Dictionary.com, s.v. "adjust," accessed May 31, 2018, http://www.dictionary.com /browse/adjust?s=t.

2. Bible Hub, s.v. "*metamorphoó*," accessed May 31, 2018, http://biblehub.com /greek/3339.htm.

3. "Michael Jordan Didn't Make Varsity—at First," *Newsweek*, October 17, 2015, www.newsweek.com/missing-cut-382954.

4. "Mia Hamm Biography," Biography, April 27, 2017, www.biography.com/people /mia-hamm-16472547.

5. Bible Hub, s.v. "*eusebeia*," accessed May 31, 2018, http://biblehub.com/greek /2150.htm.

6. Bible Hub, s.v. "*didaskalía*," "*epanorthósis*," "*paideia*," accessed May 31, 2018, http://biblehub.com/greek/1319.htm; http://biblehub.com/greek/1882.htm; http://biblehub.com/greek/3809.htm. StudyLight.org, s.v. "*elegchos*," accessed May 31, 2018, www.studylight.org/lexicons/greek/1650.html.

7. Dictionary.com, s.v. "superficial," accessed May 31, 2018, www.dictionary.com /browse/superficial?s=t.

CHAPTER 7: MAYBE CELEBRATES FREEDOM *FOR*

1. "What Does It Mean That All Things Work Together for Good?," GotQuestions. org, accessed June 4, 2018, www.gotquestions.org/all-things-work-together-for -good.html.

2. Dictionary.com, s.v. "radical," accessed June 4, 2018, www.dictionary.com/browse /radical?s=t.

3. Tebowing, accessed June 4, 2018, http://tebowing.com.

4. "Tim Tebow: Power of Prayer," ABCNews, accessed June 4, 2018, http://abcnews .go.com/Nightline/video/tim-tebow-power-prayer-15512001.

5. StudyLight.org, s.v. "*agapé*," accessed June 4, 2018, www.studylight.org/lexicons /greek/25.html.

6. StudyLight.org, s.v. "*echthros*," accessed June 4, 2018, www.studylight.org /lexicons/greek/2190.html.

7. Raquel Dunn, "Mandisa's American Idol Moment," CBN, accessed June 4, 2018, www1.cbn.com/mandisas-american-idol-moment-0.

CHAPTER 8: MAYBE CONSIDERS BEFORE COMMITTING

1. "Adrian Rogers Quotes," Christian Quotes, accessed June 4, 2018, http://christian-quotes.ochristian.com/Adrian-Rogers-Quotes/page-2.shtml.

2. Dictionary.com, s.v. "consider," accessed June 4, 2018, www.dictionary.com /browse/consider?s=t.

3. StudyLight.org, s.v. "*exagorazó*," accessed June 4, 2018, www.studylight.org /lexicons/greek/1805.html.

4. StudyLight.org, s.v. "*exagorazó*," accessed June 4, 2018, www.studylight.org /lexicons/greek/1805.html.

5. David Guzik, "Ephesians 5—Life in the Spirit," Enduring Word, accessed June 4, 2018, https://enduringword.com/bible-commentary/ephesians-5/.

6. Stephanie Samuel, "Churches' Dilemma: 80 Percent of Clock Is Inactive," *Christian Post*, June 26, 2011, www.christianpost.com/news/authors-pastors -must-go-after-lost-sheep-to-increase-church-participation-51581/.

7. Ed Stetzer, "Three Reasons People Are Not Involved in Your Church," *Outreach Magazine*, March 20, 2015, www.outreachmagazine.com/features/5791-3 -reasons-people-are-not-involved-in-your-church.html#.U5h0e8w2TOI.twitter.

8. "Oswald Chambers—March 4 Devotional," Spiritual Life Network, accessed June 4, 2018, www.thespiritlife.net/facets/corporate/75-process/process-reflection /3665-march-4-devotional-oswald-chambers.

CHAPTER 9: MAYBE CONFRONTS *WHAT IFS* AND A WARNING

1. Bible Hub, s.v. "*tēréō*," accessed June 4, 2018, http://biblehub.com/greek/5083.htm.

2. StudyLight.org, s.v. "*pistis*," accessed June 4, 2018, www.studylight.org/lexicons /greek/4102.html.

3. David Peach, "Ten Famous Christian Martyrs," What Christians Want to Know, accessed June 4, 2018, www.whatchristianswanttoknow.com/10-famous -christian-martyrs/#ixzz4yLDZ4hC2.

4. Dictionary.com, s.v. "dedicated," "dogmatic," accessed June 4, 2018, www.dictionary.com/browse/dedicated?s=t; www.dictionary.com/browse /dogmatic?s=t. Power Thesaurus, "dedicated," "dogmatic," accessed June 4, 2018, www.powerthesaurus.org/dedicated/synonyms/2; www.powerthesaurus .org/dogmatic.

5. "What Does the Bible Say about Pride?," GotQuestions.org, accessed June 4, 2018, www.gotquestions.org/pride-Bible.html.

6. Dictionary.com, s.v. "hate," accessed June 4, 2018, www.dictionary.com/browse /hate?s=t.

EPILOGUE

1. David Ruis, "We Will Dance," LyricWiki, accessed June 4, 2018, http://lyrics .wikia.com/wiki/David_Ruis:We_Will_Dance.

About the Author

Wendy is the wife of Scott, mother of Blaire and Griffin, author, speaker, and Bible study teacher. She loves lazy Sundays watching golf with her husband, thrift-store shopping with her daughter, and watching building shows with her son.

Wendy is the author of *Wait and See: Finding Peace in God's Pauses and Plans* and the *Wait and See Participant's Guide: A Six-Session Study on Waiting Well*. She is a contributing author to the *Real-Life Women's Devotional Bible*, *Encouragement for Today: Devotions for Daily Living*, *The Reason We Speak*, and *God's Purpose for Every Woman*.

She leads women all over the world to life change through her in-depth online Bible studies. Down-to-earth and transparent, Wendy teaches in a way that women feel she is speaking directly to their hearts. She has led thousands of women through her Read Thru the Word (RTW) study of the *One Year Chronological Bible*. To grow your faith and passion for God's Word, see information about Wendy's RTW class at wendypope.org/online-studies.

Her messages are filled with biblical insights but sprinkled with just the right amount of humor to help her audiences see she is a real, everyday woman. Wendy inspires her audiences to:

- make spending time in God's Word each day a priority.
- look for God working around them every day.
- view life with a God-first perspective.

To bring the message of *Yes, No, and Maybe* or another of Wendy's inspiring topics to your next event, contact speakercoordinator @proverbs31.org.

CONNECT WITH WENDY

Website: wendypope.org
Email: wendy@wendypope.org
Facebook: www.facebook.com/WendyPopeOfficial
Twitter: @wendybpope
Instagram: Wendy_Pope
Pinterest: www.pinterest.com/wendypope67

Proverbs 31
MINISTRIES

ABOUT PROVERBS 31 MINISTRIES

If you were inspired by *Yes, No, and Maybe* and desire to deepen your own personal relationship with Jesus Christ, I encourage you to connect with Proverbs 31 Ministries.

Proverbs 31 Ministries exists to be a trusted friend who will take you by the hand and walk by your side, leading you one step closer to the heart of God through:

- Free online daily devotions
- First 5 Bible study app
- Daily radio program
- Books and resources
- Online Bible studies
- COMPEL writers training, www.CompelTraining.com

To learn more about Proverbs 31 Ministries, call 877-731-4663 or visit www.Proverbs31.org.

Proverbs 31 Ministries
630 Team Rd., Suite 100
Matthews, NC 28105
www.Proverbs31.org

Bible Credits

Unless otherwise noted, all Scripture quotations are taken from HOLY BIBLE, NEW INTERNATIONAL VERSION®, NIV® Copyright © 1973, 1978, 1984, 2011 by Biblica, Inc.® Used by permission. All rights reserved worldwide.

Scripture quotations marked AMP are taken from the Amplified® Bible, copyright © 2015 by The Lockman Foundation. Used by permission. (www.Lockman.org).

Scripture quotations marked AMPC are taken from the Amplified® Bible Classic Edition, copyright © 1954, 1987 by The Lockman Foundation. Used by permission. (www.Lockman.org).

Scripture quotations marked BSB are taken from the Berean Study Bible © 2016, 2018 by Bible Hub and Berean.Bible. All rights reserved.